T0222335

Eclipse TEA Revealed

Building Plug-ins and Creating Extensions for Eclipse

Markus Duft

Apress®

Eclipse TEA Revealed: Building Plug-ins and Creating Extensions for Eclipse

Markus Duft
Peggau, Steiermark, Austria

ISBN-13 (pbk): 978-1-4842-4092-2   ISBN-13 (electronic): 978-1-4842-4093-9
https://doi.org/10.1007/978-1-4842-4093-9

Library of Congress Control Number: 2018963591

Managing Director, Apress Media LLC: Welmoed Spahr
Acquisitions Editor: Steve Anglin
Development Editor: Matthew Moodie
Coordinating Editor: Mark Powers

Cover designed by eStudioCalamar

Cover image designed by Freepik (www.freepik.com)

Distributed to the book trade worldwide by Springer Science+Business Media New York, 233 Spring Street, 6th Floor, New York, NY 10013. Phone 1-800-SPRINGER, fax (201) 348-4505, e-mail orders-ny@springer-sbm.com, or visit www.springeronline.com. Apress Media, LLC is a California LLC and the sole member (owner) is Springer Science + Business Media Finance Inc (SSBM Finance Inc). SSBM Finance Inc is a **Delaware** corporation.

For information on translations, please e-mail editorial@apress.com; for reprint, paperback, or audio rights, please email bookpermissions@springernature.com.

Apress titles may be purchased in bulk for academic, corporate, or promotional use. eBook versions and licenses are also available for most titles. For more information, reference our Print and eBook Bulk Sales web page at http://www.apress.com/bulk-sales.

Any source code or other supplementary material referenced by the author in this book is available to readers on GitHub via the book's product page, located at www.apress.com/9781484240922. For more detailed information, please visit http://www.apress.com/source-code.

Printed on acid-free paper

To my wife, Sandra,
and my children, Nadine and Leonie

Table of Contents

About the Author ix

About the Technical Reviewer xi

Acknowledgments xiii

Chapter 1: About TEA...1

The Background of TEA...1

TEA Is Born...4

The Current State of TEA...6

Chapter 2: Getting Started 9

Eclipse Setup 10

Setting Up TEA: The Quick Start 11

Setting Up TEA: The Whole Story..14

From the Official Update Site 17

From the Source Repository 19

Running and Debugging the Samples...19

Running the Samples in the IDE 24

Running the Samples Headless..26

Chapter 3: TEA Architecture 29

TEA Components...29

TEA System Components 30

TEA Engine and Context...31

Context Dependency Injection (CDI) 33

The TEA Menu 36

Creating a TEA-Enabled Eclipse Project..37

Chapter 4: Logging **45**

Using TaskingLog 46

Tasking Live View...47

Chapter 5: Tasks **53**

Naming..54

Return Values..56

Output Capturing..57

Chapter 6: TaskChains **59**

Headless vs. UI..60

Using UI to Configure a TaskChain...63

Identifying a TaskChain..65

XVFB and Friends 71

Updates 72

Configuration 73

Life Cycle 73

Headless Life Cycle 76

Chapter 7: Configuration...**79**

Configuration Sources..83

Runtime Configuration Updates 84

Chapter 8: Progress Reporting 87

The Manual Way..87

The TaskProgressEstimationService 90

Task Cancelation and State..91

Headless/Console State Handling 96

Chapter 9: Statistics 97

Enabling Statistics Reporting..97

Default and Custom Statistics..99

Chapter 10: Tasking Live View...103

Progress View vs. Tasking Live View..103

Enhancing the View..104

Chapter 11: E4 Events..109

The Event Bridge..109

Chapter 12: TEA Build Library...115

Custom Build Elements..116

P2-Related Tasks 123

Maven Integration 126

Chapter 13: EASE Integration 133

Executing EASE Scripts from TEA 134

Executing a TaskChain from EASE 137

TEA Event Triggered EASE Scripts..141

Chapter 14: LcDsl Integration 143

Integrating with TEA...145

Generating feature.xml Using LcDsl 150

Chapter 15: Further Use Cases 155

Accessing the E4 Context 155

Menu Grouping...156

Setting Up a Headless Workspace 159

Index...163

About the Author

 **Markus Duft** has been working as a Platform Architect (C/C++, Java, and Eclipse Expert) at SSI Schaefer IT Solutions for more than 12 years. His responsibilities include creating custom Eclipse IDE extensions as well as developing the whole headless build infrastructure for large-scale Eclipse-RCP-based products. In his spare time, he is developing a hobbyist OS kernel in assembler and C. He has spoken at various EclipseCon events around the world (US, France, and Germany) about Eclipse TEA, its predecessor (WAMAS Power Build), and related topics, including launch configurations. Markus has been published in the German periodical *Eclipse Magazin*.

About the Technical Reviewer

Manuel Jordan Elera is an autodidactic developer and researcher who enjoys learning new technologies for his own experiments and creating new integrations. Manuel won the Springy Award—Community Champion and Spring Champion 2013. In his little free time, he reads the Bible and composes music on his guitar. Manuel is known as dr_pompeii. He has tech-reviewed numerous books for Apress, including *Pro Spring*, 4th Edition (2014), *Practical Spring LDAP* (2013), *Pro JPA 2*, 2nd Edition (2013), and *Pro Spring Security* (2013). Read his 13 detailed tutorials about many Spring technologies, contact him through his blog at `www.manueljordanelera.blogspot.com`, and follow him on his Twitter account, `@dr_pompeii`.

Acknowledgments

A big thanks goes to SSI Schaefer IT Solutions as a whole and especially my direct management, who made it possible to create Eclipse TEA in the first place. It would not exist without the dedication to open source of my colleagues.

CHAPTER 1

About TEA

Welcome! Take a seat. Relax. Grab some coffee. (You all drink coffee, right?) I am not going to discuss too much rocket science. If you read this book's back cover, you already know that this book is about extending the Eclipse IDE[1] with additional functionality through Eclipse TEA.[2] As you make your way through the book, you will see that this can be a surprisingly simple task.

In this chapter, I will introduce Eclipse TEA and shed some light on its history.

The Background of TEA

Before I delve into the nuts and bolts of extending the Eclipse IDE, let's look at the origin of Eclipse TEA.

---

[1]http://www.eclipse.org/
[2]http://www.eclipse.org/tea/

© Markus Duft 2018
M. Duft, *Eclipse TEA Revealed*, https://doi.org/10.1007/978-1-4842-4093-9_1

A few years ago, in the good old days of Apache Ant,[3] we were engineering a large-scale logistics application. For various reasons, Eclipse RCP[4] was chosen as this application's platform. Even for server-side applications, we used the exact same setup, except without the UI parts of Eclipse RCP. This application was extremely large; it had roughly six million lines of code and was composed of approximately 650 OSGi[5] bundles.

In order to maintain metadata, such a huge application required heavy lifting by both Eclipse and the developers' hardware (at that time), and the developers themselves.

When taking into account the build system (Apache Ant) for headless builds (in other words, running a build without any UI and usually running on a server without a monitor attached in the first place), we understood the need for very lengthy and hard-to-maintain build XML files. Additionally, there were dozens of property files containing plug-in and feature versions to build and to include in update sites.

As a consequence, we had literally weeks where not a single nightly build succeeded even though workspaces in the IDEs of the developers were OK all along, meaning that builds and tests were successful. They just forgot to maintain the additional metadata (or did it wrong unknowingly). Developers never even had a chance to test nightly builds because they required a very special setup that was nearly impossible to reproduce on individual workplaces.

Another reason for the very complex and complicated build setup was our model driven approach. There were a few code generators, which were building upon code in the workspace; these generated code with input from some projects into other projects. This required us to do the following:

---

[3]https://ant.apache.org/
[4]https://wiki.eclipse.org/Rich_Client_Platform
[5]https://www.osgi.org/

- Build shared platform projects

- Build the code generator projects

- Run the code generator(s)

- Build the projects containing the generated code

- Build more code generators, requiring the projects with previously generated code

- Generate even more code

- Build the projects containing the additional code

Eclipse does allow adding additional builders per project, but this is not what we wanted. We required some orchestration on top of the normal build process since the generators had multiple source projects, multiple input projects, and multiple output projects.

In the IDE, the developer performed this orchestration. Usually, Eclipse performed the automatic build until the first bits were compiled. (In this state, the workspace was basically full of compile errors due to missing generated code in all other projects.) Now generators could be run manually to provide the next bits of code to compile. This process was repeated until all generators had been run—a tedious job. In the headless builds, there were Apache Ant scripts, which basically did the same. Due to frequent changes in projects setups (new, removed, renamed projects, and so on), these scripts were basically always out of sync with reality.

Things continued this way until some developers had enough. They had the idea to provide some automation to the most annoying steps in the process, along with simplifying headless setups. This was the birth of WPoB—short for WAMAS (the product's name) Power Build. It was later rewritten and rebranded as Eclipse TEA.

TEA Is Born

The initial idea of TEA was to be able to do the following:

- Build our software without additional configuration files or build scripts so developers cannot fail to maintain them

- Run all code generators at the right point in time, automatically discovering projects, dependencies, and so on

- Do both of the above in the Eclipse Workspace as well as headless on any machine without additional setup

Initially, TEA was basically a wrapper and tiny orchestrator around the IProject.build() method, already provided by Eclipse. Thus, anything hooked on the default Eclipse mechanism for extending the build worked out of the box, but TEA was able to provide the additional orchestration on top.

As a positive side effect, which was discovered during implementation, a remarkable performance gain occurred once the first version of TEA was able to build our workspace. As of the time of writing, developers use the TEA mechanisms to build the workspace instead of the automatic build in case there are a lot of changes to be compiled—for instance, when updating the workspace with a lot of changes from the source repository.

The reason for this performance gain (today it is not as huge as it was back then) was traced back to the fact that Eclipse does not have an orchestration on top of the individual project builds. Eclipse has a build order for the workspace that may be good—but may be just as bad. The developer can manually set up the order, or it can be left up to Eclipse to calculate it (which is the default). Eclipse accounts for multiple factors when trying to figure out a build order such as project dependencies and references. In our case, it seemed to come up with a rather bad order that resulted in Eclipse running in circles trying to compile certain projects over and over again, although their prerequisite projects were not yet compiled. Along with our generators, which interrupted the build process multiple times along the way, there was no chance to find a good ordering any way in the first place.

Eclipse TEA's build library does not have this problem. It adds an orchestrator that calculates a graph up front, allowing for manipulating and influencing this graph. Other than Eclipse's build order, this graph cannot be influenced by configuration of Eclipse. However, it can be extended and manipulated via code. I will provide a detailed description of this mechanism later in this book.

But there is more. Looking at the current open source Ecosystem, reading mailing lists, and so on, you will likely discover mails discussing how to prevent the fact that certain ways of working break things for others working in a different way. For example, projects where half the developers use Eclipse and the other half does not fall into this category. Headless builds are also usually performed without Eclipse (they are rather performed by tools like Apache Maven,[6] Gradle,[7] and so on), so the ones avoiding Eclipse all together might easily break things for the others. In this case, it can help to have an additional build performed using Eclipse, which is a simple task using Eclipse TEA.

What I have described so far is actually only an optional part of today's Eclipse TEA (called "Eclipse TEA build library"). The core of TEA was a byproduct of our initial efforts to get the builds, as previously described.

To be able to encapsulate the individual steps of the builds (building, generating code, and so on), a rudimentary task-based execution engine was implemented. It had the capability to execute a `TaskChain`, which configured a series of certain `Task` objects to be executed. The concepts of

---

[6]https://maven.apache.org/
[7]https://gradle.org/

`Task` and `TaskChain` are at the heart of TEA and are mentioned in all of the subsequent chapters.

Building upon these concepts, we implemented the things we wanted to perform in the IDE or in headless environments as tasks. This implementation paid off more than once because it was easy to reuse tasks in headless environments.

The Current State of TEA

Today we have `Tasks` (listed in no particular order) that perform the following:

- Update the running Eclipse installation automatically

- Clone and import repositories

- Set up a workspace (import projects)

- Set up a target platform

- Configure preferences in the workspace automatically

- Build all projects

- Launch any launch configuration (for example, external programs, generators, and so on)

- Generate `feature.xml` files for update sites

- Export JAR files and build update sites from them

- Build and export Eclipse products (`.zip`) from the update sites

- Generate and export documentation in various formats, including dependency graphs, database model reports, and so forth

- Run tests, including UI tests distributed among multiple virtual machines

- Run "FindBugs"

- Integrate with external systems like "SonarQube" and others

- Run code generators, code formatters, and code cleanup

Now that I have told you what is possible, I must inform you that not all of this is (yet) in the open source Eclipse TEA. A lot of this code is still closed source (but there is the intention to open source everything which is not too specific to the company—meaning everything that does not hard code concepts of the software we are building).

I include it here so you can get a picture of what is feasible to be implemented using Eclipse TEA.

CHAPTER 2

Getting Started

To begin developing Eclipse extensions using TEA, you will need an Eclipse Workspace with a target platform configured to include TEA. The target platform in Eclipse defines the target environment to compile for. We want to develop components for TEA, thus the Eclipse IDE and TEA have to be defined as our target platform. The easiest way to achieve this is to install a TEA workspace using the Eclipse installer. You can also install TEA into an existing Eclipse installation and use the Running Platform target. Note that this is not (always) recommended for production setups since the Running Platform may not be stable across setups. (In other words, a developer might want to install additional software. In this case, the developer could write code that references the code installed in their private Eclipse installation, which will not work for any other developer.) It is always a good idea to have a well-defined target platform.

At the time of writing, TEA requires at least Java 8 (and is tested up to Java 10), and it requires a target platform that includes PDE and JDT—that is, you need to install an according Eclipse package. I recommend either Eclipse for RCP and RAP Developers or Eclipse IDE for Eclipse Committers. It is not mandatory to use one of them, but they contain everything required from the start. I will use the latter one for all the samples in this book. If you want to use a different setup, you can do so as long as the required parts (PDE, JDT, and Launch Configuration View[1]) are installed. TEA should run equally well on those setups.

---

[1] http://marketplace.eclipse.org/content/launch-configuration-view

© Markus Duft 2018
M. Duft, *Eclipse TEA Revealed*, https://doi.org/10.1007/978-1-4842-4093-9_2

Eclipse Setup

Download the Eclipse Installer from the official Eclipse website,[2] as shown in Figure 2-1.

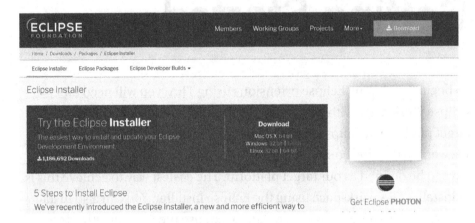

Figure 2-1. *Eclipse download*

Use the downloaded installer to set up an Eclipse installation. (As previously mentioned, I will go with the Eclipse IDE for Eclipse Committers.) I will be using the advanced mode since it allows us to directly set up a TEA workspace from within the Eclipse installer. To enable the Advanced Mode, click the options button in the upper-right corner of the installer and select Advanced Mode..., as shown in Figure 2-2.

---

[2]http://www.eclipse.org/downloads/packages/installer

Figure 2-2. *Switch to Advanced Mode*

Setting Up TEA: The Quick Start

If you want to get started really quickly, you can use the Eclipse installer to do all the required setup steps, clone repositories, and so on. Once in advanced mode, confirm the Eclipse IDE for Eclipse Committers selection and the Eclipse version (I tested with Eclipse Photon), as shown in Figure 2-3.

Figure 2-3. *Advanced Eclipse installation*

In the next step, you can select a project you want to work on. In this case, make sure to select Eclipse TEA, as shown in Figure 2-4.

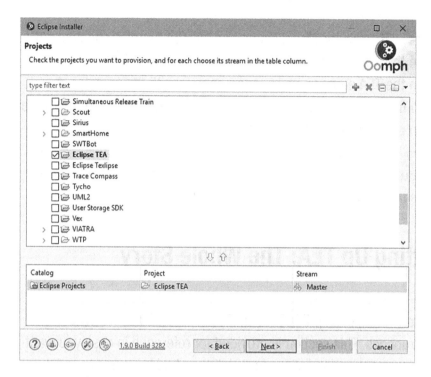

Figure 2-4. *Choose to set up Eclipse TEA workspace*

The last page of the installer allows you to tweak the setup even more (for example, the installation folder). No changes are required to get started, so you can confirm the defaults and finish the wizard.

Note   The quick start will provide you with a "good" setup, using a dedicated target platform instead of using `Running Platform`. It includes all required components to get you started.

The wizard will start the resulting Eclipse installation in order to finish setting up the workspace. This will take a few seconds. Unfortunately, the only indication of the work being done is a tiny spinning icon in the status bar at the bottom of the Eclipse window. However, you can click this icon to see a more detailed version of the progress.

> **Note**   The resulting workspace has the TEA bundles checked out
> from the source repository. This is a good setup to look up things
> from the TEA sources while experimenting with the samples. A
> recommended production setup would have TEA provided as binaries
> from a target platform[3] instead.

You should now have a working Eclipse installation running on a
workspace with the Eclipse TEA projects already present.

Setting Up TEA: The Whole Story

> **Note**   You can skip this section if you followed the previous
> instructions. This section is provided for reference in case you want
> to reuse an existing Eclipse installation or build one from scratch.

Using the manual route, there are two ways of getting started with
TEA: using binaries from the official update site, or cloning and importing
the TEA source repository. Both methods should lead to comparable
results—the second one being quite close to the quick start variant.
Using the source repository has the advantage of being able to look at the
source code of TEA more easily. The downside is that you need to have
all dependencies to build TEA available from the target platform (that is,
installed into your Eclipse when using the Running Platform target). It is
also not recommended to have the TEA source code in a workspace where
you develop components for production use.

---

[3]Read more about target platforms in general at https://help.eclipse.org/
photon/topic/org.eclipse.pde.doc.user/concepts/target.htm

Note   In both setup scenarios, you need EASE to install TEA's EASE support libraries. EASE consists of a lot of components for different scripting languages. I suggest (keeping the set small in the beginning) installing the following features from the update site `http://download.eclipse.org/ease/update/release` by clicking Help ➤ Install new Software and pasting the URL:

EASE Core Framework

EASE UI Components

EASE Jython Support

I used EASE version 0.6.0 to test the samples. (See Figure 2-5.)

Figure 2-5. *Install EASE from the official update site*

Note   The same method can be used for LcDsl, which you will need that later on. Install LcDsl from the updated site: `https://mduft.github.io/lcdsl-latest/`. I suggest installing both features:

Launch Configuration DSL

Launch Configuration View

(See Figure 2-6.)

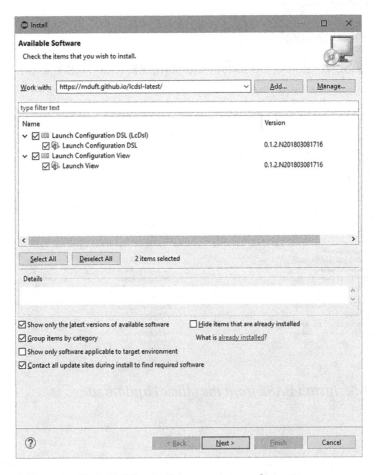

Figure 2-6. *Install LcDsl from the current update site*

From the Official Update Site

You can install TEA from the official P2 Update Site into Eclipse by visiting the Eclipse Marketplace (`https://marketplace.eclipse.org/content/eclipse-tea-tasking-engine-advanced`). Follow the instructions on the page, either drag the Install button to the IDE or copy and paste the update site URL into the Help ➤ Install New Software... dialog. Figure 2-7 shows how to install from the TEA update site.

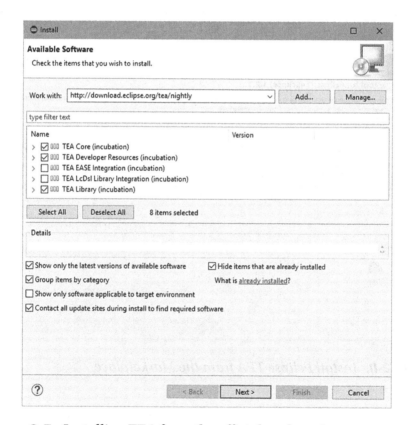

Figure 2-7. *Installing TEA from the official update site*

Alternatively, you can use the Eclipse Marketplace client as well (`Help > Eclipse Marketplace...`), as shown in Figure 2-8.

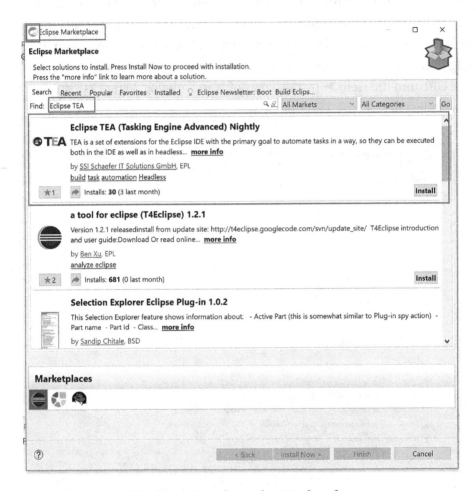

Figure 2-8. *Install Eclipse TEA from the Marketplace*

From the Source Repository

As previously mentioned, you will have to have EASE and LcDsl available from the target platform.

1. Install them from the previous URLs into Eclipse if you are using the `Running Platform` target platform.

2. Make sure that both are available from your target platform if you use an explicit one.

3. Clone their repositories into your workspace and make sure the required parts are available.

4. Once you have made EASE and LcDsl available, you can find the TEA repository on the official Eclipse Gerrit server: `https://git.eclipse.org/r/#/ admin/projects/tea/tea`.

Running and Debugging the Samples

The book is accompanied by a sample repository,[4] containing all the sample code discussed in the book. Let's now add the sample repository to the workspace by cloning it.

Open the `Git Repositories` view, as shown in Figure 2-9.

---

[4]`https://github.com/apress/eclipse-tea-revealed`

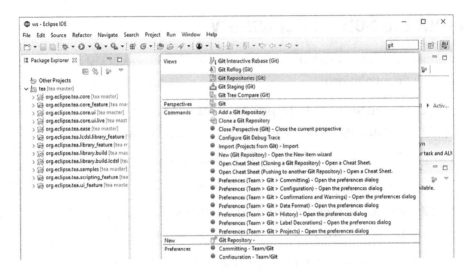

Figure 2-9. *Open Git Repositories view*

You will see the TEA repository in the list. Now add the sample repository. Click the Clone a Git repository and add it to this view button from the view's toolbar. In the Clone Git Repository wizard, select Clone URI and click Next, as shown in Figure 2-10.

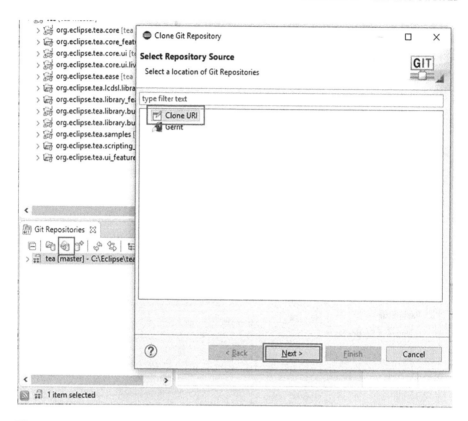

Figure 2-10. *Open the Clone Git Repository wizard*

On the following page, enter the repository URL previously given and click Next. See Figure 2-11.

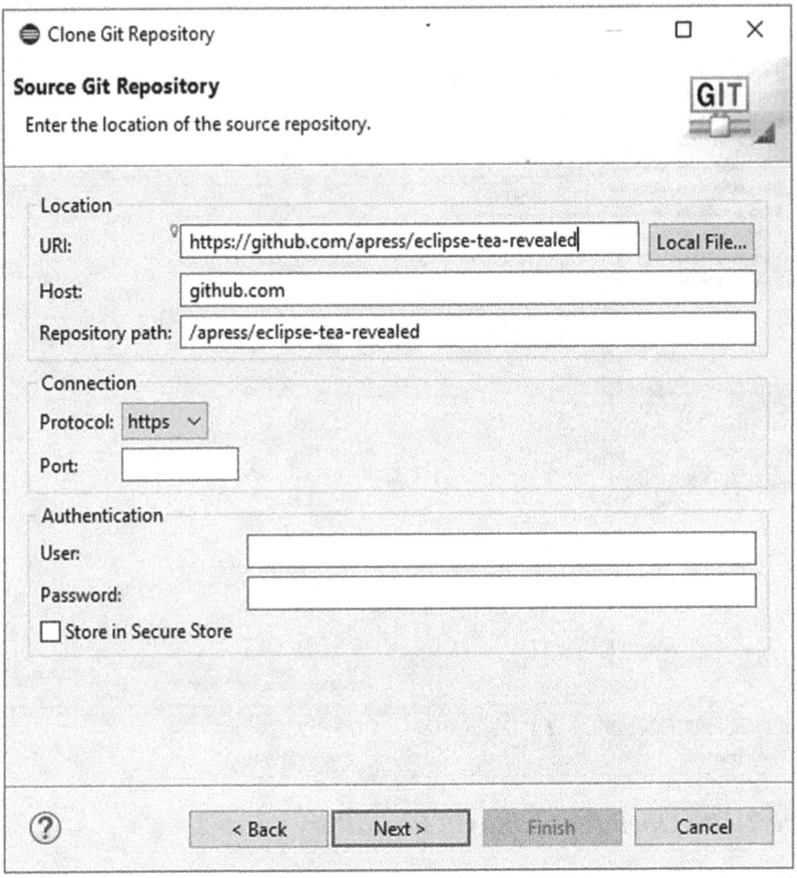

Figure 2-11. *Enter sample repository URL*

Simply confirm the following page (selecting all branches). On the last page, you can modify the target directory on your local machine. However, you don't have to. The default is inside your home directory, which is fine.

After you click Finish, the repository is cloned and will appear in the Git Repositories view. The last step is to right-click the repository and select Import Projects... to import the sample projects. Import all of them, as shown in Figure 2-12.

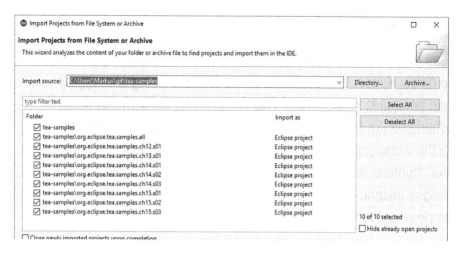

Figure 2-12. *Import projects*

Confirm the selection by clicking Finish. All sample projects are now imported into the workspace. Now you're good to go!

All samples are available, so let's take a look at how to run them. Since TEA is all about running the same tasks both in the IDE as well as headless, we will run them both ways. We will start with the simplest TaskChain in the org.eclipse.tea.samples.ch02.s01 project. Executing the TaskChain will do nothing more than display "Hello World" on the screen. It will do so using the TaskingLog (we will discuss it later), which transparently logs either to the command line (headless) or the Tasking Console view. (In the IDE, think "Runtime Workspace.")

You can take a look around in the project and explore the actual source code, but for now I want to focus on how to run the sample instead of its content. (I guess "Hello World" can be achieved in a multitude of different ways as well.)

Note   A word on the "Runtime Workspace": We will be developing (and test-driving) Eclipse IDE extensions. We will be using Eclipse to do so. Hence, the "application" we are developing (debugging and testing) is Eclipse itself. This can cause quite some confusion. Whenever I'm talking about the "TEA Workspace," I am referring to the workspace you just prepared. Whenever I'm talking about the "Runtime Workspace," I am referring to the workspace in the Eclipse instance(s) that we will be launching from within the "TEA Workspace" to test our code.

Running the Samples in the IDE

TEA uses LcDsl to define launch configurations. This means that launch configurations are defined in .lc files. From these files, Eclipse launch configurations are generated as required on the fly. Our first sample project contains such a file: org.eclipse.tea.samples.ch02.s01/launch.lc Listing 2-1 shows its contents.

Listing 2-1. First Sample's launch.lc File

```
eclipse configuration CH02-IDE {
        product org.eclipse.sdk.ide;

        feature org.eclipse.tea.core_feature;
        feature org.eclipse.tea.ui_feature;

        feature org.eclipse.sdk;

        plugin org.eclipse.tea.samples.ch02.s01;

        workspace "${workspace_loc}/runtime-ws/ch02";
}
```

```
eclipse configuration CH02-Headless : CH02-IDE {
        product org.eclipse.tea.core.ui.HeadlessTaskingEngine;

        argument "-taskchain" "FirstTaskChain";

        workspace "${workspace_loc}/runtime-ws/ch02-hl";
}
```

These configurations[5] will also appear in the Launch Configurations view, as shown in Figure 2-13.

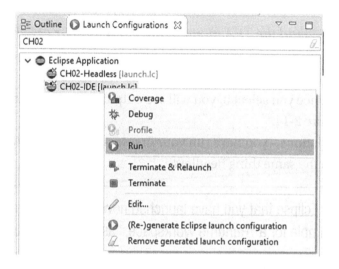

Figure 2-13. *Running the sample launch from the view*

As shown in Figure 2-13, right-click the CH02-IDE launch configuration and select Run from the context menu. An Eclipse will be launched, containing all the required plug-ins for the sample. You can find the TEA top-level menu in the IDE's main menu bar seen in Figure 2-14.

---

[5]Read more about how LcDsl works here: `https://github.com/mduft/lcdsl`

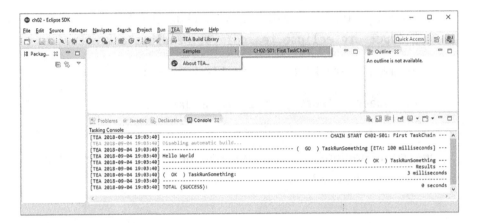

Figure 2-14. *Find the TEA menu in the main toolbar of Eclipse*

Click the menu bar and find the Samples ➤ CH02-S01: First TaskChain menu item. Once you select it, you will see output in the Console view, as shown in Figure 2-14.

Congratulations—you have run your first sample! Now let's take a look at how to run the same thing headless.

Note   The Eclipse that you have launched now to run the sample is the first example for a "Runtime Workspace," as previously mentioned.

Now you can simply close this Eclipse instance and return to the TEA Workspace to move on to the headless execution.

Running the Samples Headless

The samples contain another launch configuration, which allows running the same thing without IDE. TEA allows two different headless modes of operation:

- Using the Eclipse application `org.eclipse.tea.core.TaskingEngine`[6]

- Using the Eclipse product `org.eclipse.tea.core.ui.HeadlessTaskingEngine`[7]

The difference between the two is that the first one is very slim and will not require very much dependency-wise. The second one has more dependencies, but it allows running (almost) any code from plug-ins with UI dependencies. It starts a headless presentation engine that will fake an E4[8]-based IDE workbench. This trick is borrowed from the Eclipse unit tests.

The launch configuration `CH02-Headless` will run the same `TaskChain` as before, but by using a dedicated application. Instead of opening another Eclipse instance ("Runtime Workspace"), you will see the output in the Console view of the TEA Workspace this time. It behaves exactly as any other application launched from any Eclipse, as shown in Figure 2-15.

---

[6]Implemented in the class `org.eclipse.tea.core.internal.TaskingEngineApplication`

[7]Implemented in the class `org.eclipse.tea.core.ui.internal.TaskingEngineExtendedApplication`

[8]E4 is the name of the new APIs introduced with Eclipse 4+

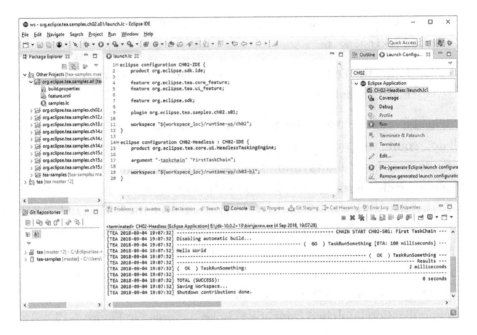

Figure 2-15. *Executing the same sample with the headless application*

You might notice that there is a little more console output, compared to the previous execution (inside the Runtime Workspace). This is due to the fact that TEA needs to setup (and clean up) an IDE-like environment, so that any TaskChain executed can access Eclipse components that would not be available otherwise.

CHAPTER 3

TEA Architecture

Now that we have finished verifying the Eclipse installation and workspace setup, let's look at the architecture of TEA. It is important to understand the key concepts and design decisions in TEA because you will use the very same architecture to extend TEA and develop your own components.

TEA Components

TEA builds on two major concepts:

- E4 Context Dependency Injection

- OSGi Services (using SCR annotations)

OSGi services are used to find participating components in the system, and E4's Context Dependency Injection framework (DI) is used to interact with those components. Figure 3-1 shows how these technologies are used by TEA.

© Markus Duft 2018
M. Duft, *Eclipse TEA Revealed*, https://doi.org/10.1007/978-1-4842-4093-9_3

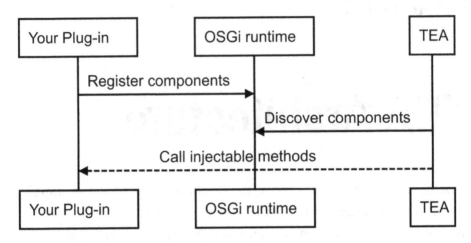

Figure 3-1. *How TEA uses OSGi services and contexts and dependency injection*

> **Note**   TEA usually does not create instances of components itself; thus, constructor dependency injection is typically not supported. The OSGi runtime is responsible for providing properly initialized service instances. This also means that components can use the usual service dependency and activation mechanisms—like any other OSGi service.

In subsequent chapters, you will learn how to contribute custom TEA components, as described in Figure 3-1. In fact, this is why you are reading this in the first place.

TEA System Components

TEA consists of quite a few system components. Figure 3-2 shows an overview of them. Each of the components will be explained in the book, so don't worry if not everything is clear just by looking at the picture.

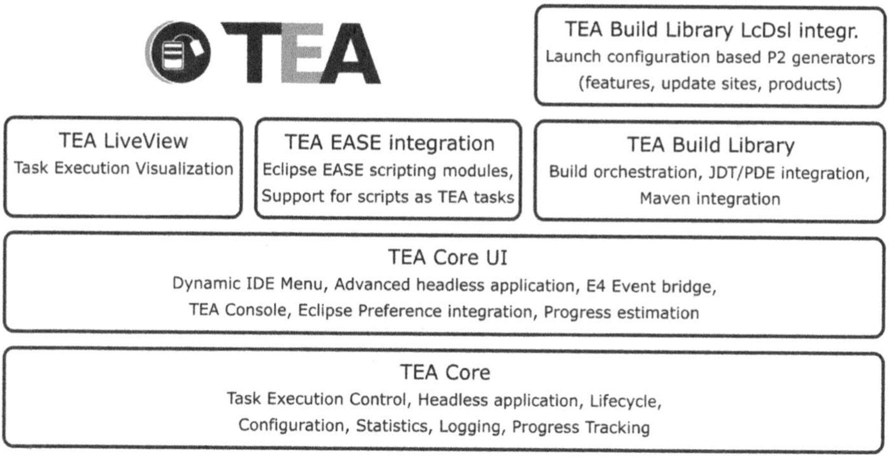

	TEA Build Library LcDsl integr.
	Launch configuration based P2 generators (features, update sites, products)

TEA LiveView	TEA EASE integration	TEA Build Library
Task Execution Visualization	Eclipse EASE scripting modules, Support for scripts as TEA tasks	Build orchestration, JDT/PDE integration, Maven integration

TEA Core UI
Dynamic IDE Menu, Advanced headless application, E4 Event bridge,
TEA Console, Eclipse Preference integration, Progress estimation

TEA Core
Task Execution Control, Headless application, Lifecycle,
Configuration, Statistics, Logging, Progress Tracking

Figure 3-2. *Overview of all TEA system components*

We will mostly focus on the lower two layers (TEA Core UI and TEA Core) first because the other layers cover more advanced topics.

TEA Engine and Context

To understand the architecture of TEA, you must know the components involved, their task in the system, and how they are linked together. A picture tells more than a thousand words, so I've heard. I will nevertheless explain the Figure 3-3 a little bit.

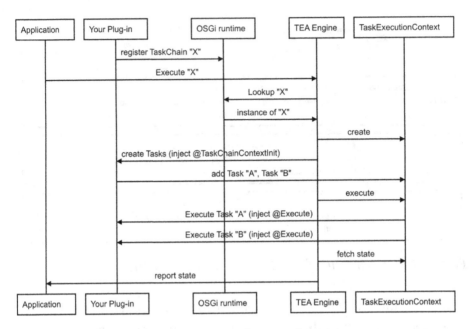

Figure 3-3. *TEA system component interaction*

At startup, a plug-in registers its TEA component implementations with the OSGi runtime. This typically happens transparently because TEA uses the Declarative Services (DS) annotations for the Service Component Runtime (SCR).

Once all plug-ins have started up, an application can request the TEA Engine—the part of TEA responsible for actually running your components—to execute a certain TaskChain ("X"). This can be either the IDE (when a user clicks an entry in the TEA menu) or the headless application when executing the TaskChain passed by ID. The engine will query the OSGi runtime for according component registrations. Once an instance for a TaskChain has been found, a TaskExecutionContext for this execution cycle is created. This context is passed to the discovered TaskChain instance for initialization.

Now the TaskChain implementation is responsible for telling the
TaskExecutionContext which Task objects exist and should be executed.
Task objects are visited in the order added to the context.

Note   It is possible to nest TaskChain implementations by using
the TaskLazyChainWrapper Task object. Wrapped TaskChain
implementations are initialized lazily and allow reacting on results of
other Tasks during TaskChain initialization, which is not possible
otherwise.

Now that an initialized TaskExecutionContext exists, the TEA Engine
will request its execution, which will in turn visit all registered Task objects
in it. Task objects are normalized first (in other words, if you registered
a Class object, an instance of it will be created by the engine) and then
run by executing the method annotated with @Execute using the E4
dependency injection framework.

Context Dependency Injection (CDI)

TEA uses dependency injection (inversion of control) throughout all of its
components. It is used to provide anything a Task or TaskChain needs to it.

The big advantage of CDI is the flexibility in the signatures of
interfaces and methods. Nearly no interface in TEA defines actual
methods. Usually, TEA finds components and executes annotated
methods on them (using DI).

This means that a component can request any object to be injected
when calling its annotated methods, without the need to change TEA's
interface to accommodate it.

For example, suppose there is a (hypothetical) interface SomeService
in TEA, as shown in Listing 3-1.

Listing 3-1. TEA Component Marker Interface

```
/**
 * Some TEA component interface
 */
public interface SomeInterface {
}
```

This interface has not a single method defined. Usually, the documentation of the interface will state which types of annotated methods are supported. If none are mentioned, @Execute is the default annotation.

A typical implementation for such a component interface would look like the code snippet in Listing 3-2.

Listing 3-2. Sample TEA Component Implementation

```
import org.eclipse.e4.core.di.annotations.Execute;
import org.eclipse.tea.core.services.TaskingLog;
import org.osgi.service.component.annotations.Component;

@Component
public class SomeImpl implements SomeInterface {
    @Execute
    public void myMethod(TaskingLog log) {
        log.info("Hello TEA");
    }
}
```

There are a few things worth noting here:

- The @Component annotation (explained in more detail in the next chapter): It will make sure that the component is registered as OSGi service and discovered by TEA when it is looking for implementations of SomeInterface.

- The @Execute annotation on myMethod: When TEA
  processes SomeInterface implementations, it will
  use E4's context dependency injection framework to
  execute an annotated method (explicitly stating which
  annotation must be present on the method to match)
  using the current context.

- The TaskingLog instance in the methods signature: The
  DI framework will make sure on its own, based on the
  current context, which instance is filled in. In this case,
  TEA will fail if there is no TaskingLog available, since
  the parameter is not marked with @Optional.

I have mentioned context a few times. What is the current context (not
to be confused with the TaskExecutionContext, which is not related to
dependency injection directly)? Well, it depends. Services implementing
life cycle hooks will have a much smaller context (for instance, while the
application is starting up, there is not much context information available)
than services implementing a TaskChain. Figure 3-4 shows the available
levels of contexts created by TEA and where they are typically available.

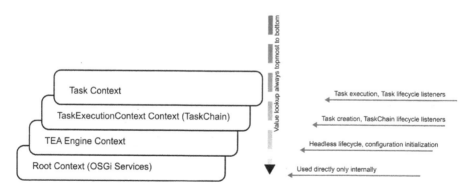

Figure 3-4. *DI context nesting*

Depending on the context, different things can be injected. There are some things that TEA provides on its own (discussed in detail throughout the rest of the book). And then there are things you can provide on your own by storing them in the context. This can be used to pass values to other Tasks in the same TaskChain, for instance.

In Listing 3-2, you saw a sample implementation of a hypothetical TEA component. The implementation class is annotated with the @Component annotation. What does it do? It is quite special. The annotation belongs to the so-called declarative services (DS), and is leveraged by the service component runtime (SCR).

Briefly described, this is an OSGi component, which will make sure that services are activated (and deactivated) at the right point in time, taking into account dependencies to other services.

Now, what is so special about the @Component annotation, which will make sure that the implementation is registered with this SCR?

It is a compile-time annotation. A generator in Eclipse will find and leverage this annotation to generate XML descriptors (which in turn are picked up by SCR at runtime) to register the implementation.

Since this requires the generator to run (and it is not the default), some setup steps for Eclipse TEA extension projects need to be performed, which I describe in more detail momentarily when I talk about setting up a TEA enabled project.

The TEA Menu

The dynamic TEA menu allows access to all available TaskChain implementations registered with the system. There is a lot of information throughout the book on how to influence the content and appearance of this menu. Figure 3-5 shows some sample content. You will likely see similar menu contents during your first tests.

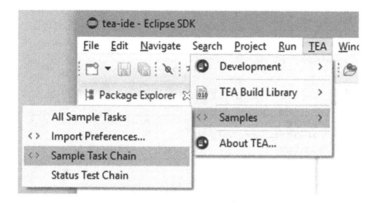

Figure 3-5. *The dynamic TEA menu*

Creating a TEA-Enabled Eclipse Project

To start implementing TEA components, you will require a Plug-in
Project. You can create it by using Eclipse's File ➤ New ➤ Project... menu.

Note   It is important to create the project in the TEA Workspace (the
workspace you are developing TEA extensions in), not in a runtime
workspace. (See Chapter 2 for more information.)

Choose Plug-in Project as type and click Next, as demonstrated in
Figure 3-6.

Figure 3-6. *Create a new Plug-in Project*

Provide a good name for the project, as shown in Figure 3-7. You may also look at the rest of the settings (I'm generous, right?), but no further changes are really required for TEA. Click Next.

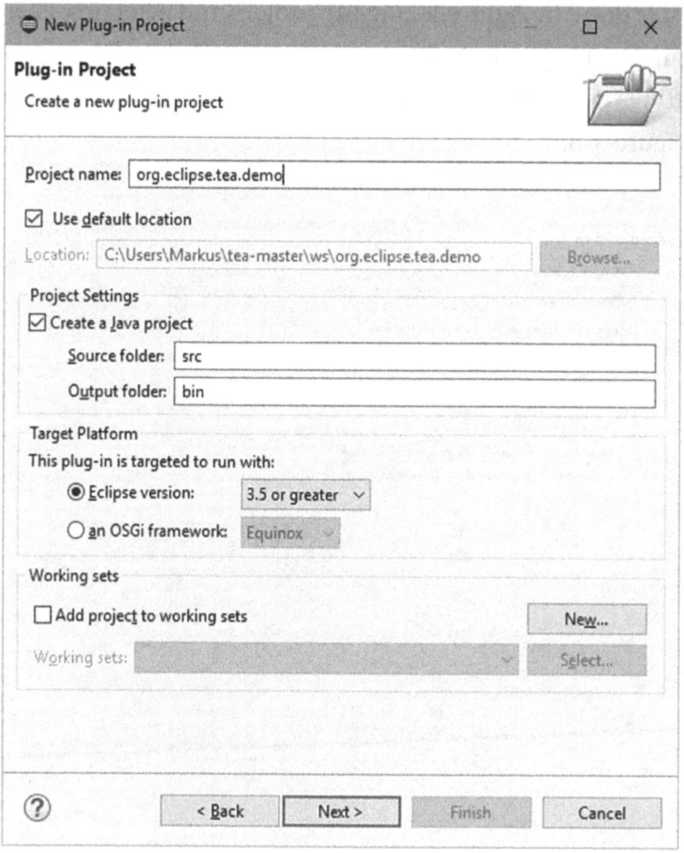

Figure 3-7. *General project settings*

On the final page, no modifications are explicitly required—you can, of course, set the execution environment. As noted before, at least Java 8 is required, and up to Java 10 is tested. Click Finish to create the project.

We will need to set up two things:

1. Support for the @Component annotation (and other DS annotations[1])

2. Dependencies to TEA and dependency injection bundles

---

[1]https://osgi.org/specification/osgi.cmpn/7.0.0/service.component.html

The first is done by right-clicking the project and selecting Properties. Go to Plug-in Development ➤ DS Annotations and check Enable project-specific settings as well as Generate descriptors from annotated sources, as shown in Figure 3-8.

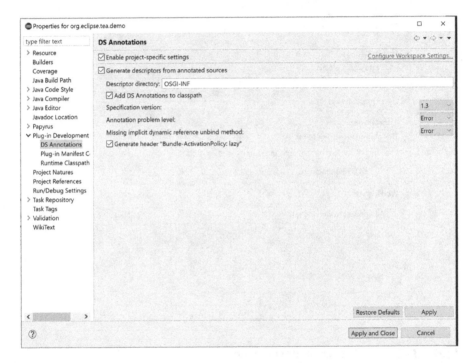

Figure 3-8. *Enable DS annotations*

You can also change this setting workspace-wide under Window ➤ Preferences, but I suggest configuring it per project since otherwise the project might not work in a workspace that is set up differently. And by "might not work," I mean that the plug-in will compile perfectly fine, but services may or may not be registered and/or found. If a workspace is not configured to generate the annotated component's descriptors as expected, it will simply not generate descriptors for newly added services. These services will be ignored at runtime because there is no descriptor that makes the service known to the runtime.

For our first experiments with TEA, it will be sufficient to add only two dependencies to the plug-in, as shown in Figure 3-9—use the Add... button in the plug-ins `MANIFEST.MF` (the editor for this file is opened automatically after creating the project) to open a dialog where you can choose the bundles to add dependencies to.

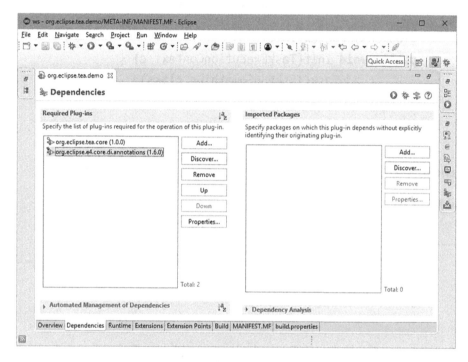

Figure 3-9. *Required basic dependencies*

Completing these steps will leave you with a skeleton project. Now you need to fill it with TEA components. To get you started, let's fill the skeleton with at least a little life. Take a look at the two classes in Listing 3-3 and Listing 3-4. Paste the code into your project.

Listing 3-3. TaskChainRunSomething.java

```
@TaskChainId(description = "My First TaskChain")
@TaskChainMenuEntry(path = "Samples")
@Component
public class TaskChainRunSomething
                        implements TaskChain {

    @TaskChainContextInit
    public void init(TaskExecutionContext c) {
        c.addTask(TaskRunSomething.class);
    }

}
```

Listing 3-4. TaskRunSomething.java

```
public class TaskRunSomething {

    @Execute
    public void run(TaskingLog log) {
        log.info("Hello World");
    }

}
```

Now that you want to try it out, you may ask yourself how to actually run it. TEA usually uses LcDsl to define launch configurations, so let's do the same thing here. Create a new file named launch.lc at the root of the project, as shown in Figure 3-10. Be sure to confirm the question regarding the Xtext nature with Yes.

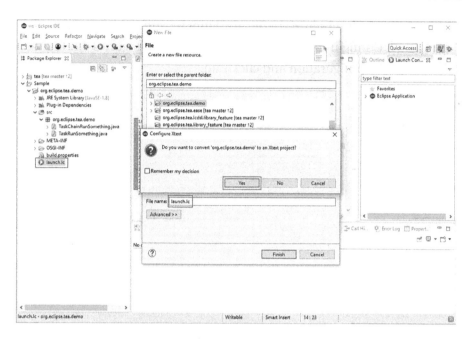

Figure 3-10.   *Create a* launch.lc *file*

Now fill in the file with the launch configuration outlined in Listing 3-5. It will start a simple Eclipse IDE with not much in it, except your first plug-in (and your first TaskChain).

Listing 3-5.   A Simple Eclipse Launch Configuration Using LcDsl (launch.lc)

```
eclipse configuration MyDemo-IDE {
    product org.eclipse.sdk.ide;
    feature org.eclipse.tea.core_feature;
    feature org.eclipse.tea.ui_feature;
    feature org.eclipse.sdk;

    plugin org.eclipse.tea.demo;

    workspace "${workspace_loc}/runtime/my-sample";
}
```

Once you save the launch.lc file, the launch configuration will appear in the Launch Configurations view. You can see this in Figure 3-11. Right-click the launch configuration and click Run.

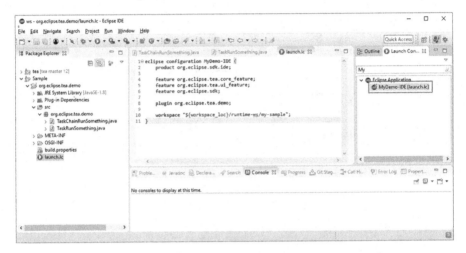

Figure 3-11. *The new launch configuration from* launch.lc *to run the demo*

A second Eclipse will open up now. Switch to it, close the Welcome page, and click TEA ➤ Samples ➤ My First TaskChain, as shown in Figure 3-12. You will be rewarded with the output depicted in Figure 3-12 as well.

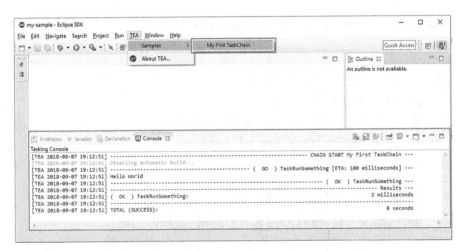

Figure 3-12. *The first* TaskChain *sample in your plug-in*

CHAPTER 4

Logging

TEA uses a custom logging mechanism called TaskingLog. The mechanism uses OSGi services to plug implementations of logging back ends. Currently, there are two back ends—one for IDE (UI) and one for headless operation. It is important to understand that the goal is not to be integrated or compatible with other logging frameworks; this is intentional. The aim is only to provide a mechanism to write logs to a single destination and place them where they are needed—in a view inside the IDE and on the console during headless execution.

The headless back end simply logs to stdout/stderr. The implementation can be found (for reference) in org.eclipse.tea. core.internal.DefaultTaskingLog.

The UI implementation can be found in org.eclipse.tea.core. ui.TaskingConsole. TEA provides a custom console implementation— the Tasking Console. You will use it frequently in the next chapters. This console is created automatically when required. You just need to have the default Eclipse Console view open. Have a look at Figure 4-1 for an example. The code to produce this output has already been covered in Listing 3-4.

```
[Problems  Javadoc  Declaration  Console 23                                                                        
Tasking Console
[TEA 2018-06-21 08:45:22] ------------------------------------------------------------------- CHAIN START Sample Task Chain ---
[TEA 2018-06-21 08:45:22] Disabling automatic build...
[TEA 2018-06-21 08:45:22] -------------------------------------------------- (  GO  ) SampleSimpleTask [ETA: 100 milliseconds] ---
[TEA 2018-06-21 08:45:22] Hello World
[TEA 2018-06-21 08:45:22] ------------------------------------------------------------------------ (  OK  ) SampleSimpleTask ---
[TEA 2018-06-21 08:45:22] ------------------------------------------------------------------------------------------- Results ---
[TEA 2018-06-21 08:45:22] (  OK  ) SampleSimpleTask:                                                            22 milliseconds
[TEA 2018-06-21 08:45:22] -----------------------------------------------------------------------------------------------------
[TEA 2018-06-21 08:45:22] TOTAL (SUCCESS):                                                                         0 seconds
```

Figure 4-1. *The default TaskingLog implementation in the IDE uses the Eclipse Console view*

Using TaskingLog

The TaskingLog is a somewhat special TEA service. It is created as soon as it is requested the first time (through the TaskingLogLookupContextFunction). It is possible to add custom implementations of TaskingLog to override the default behavior, even though this was never required until now. The Console view is usually fine in the IDE, and a third-party tool such as Jenkins[1] will usually capture the output in the headless case. The TaskingLogLookupContextFunction will use the first available implementation that is suitable for the current mode of operation (headless vs. UI). The @TaskingLogQualifier annotation will determine whether a custom implementation is suitable for the current mode.

Due to the early availability (also during startup of the application), this is a good example of something you can obtain using dependency injection in any custom component implementation. A sample Task implementation that does this is shown in Listing 4-1.

The API of TaskingLog itself is simplistic, but comparable to other logger implementations for Java (though there is no interoperability built-in intentionally). Methods for logging with different severities exist. The only thing worth mentioning is that, apart from the normal logging

---

[1]https://jenkins.io/

methods, it allows for directly accessing the streams used to log for certain levels. As a result, output of code that is not aware of TaskingLog can write there using a standard java.io.PrintStream. TEA usually formats all log output by prefixing it with the current time. This can be avoided by using the streams directly.

Listing 4-1 shows some examples of how to use the TaskingLog. If you are familiar with other logging APIs, you will not have any problems.

Listing 4-1. Sample TaskingLog Usage

```
public class TaskRunSomething {

    @Execute
    public void run(TaskingLog log) {
        log.info("Hello World");
        log.error("Something happened",
            new RuntimeException("Oops"));

        log.warn().println(
            "Direct stream access");
        log.warn().println(
            "No formatting and tagging!");
    }

}
```

Tasking Live View

Another sort of logging is the Tasking Live View. Figure 4-2 shows how it displays TaskChain and Task objects executed by TEA. There will be more information on this view in Chapter 10.

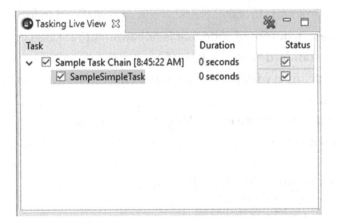

Figure 4-2. *Tasking Live View showing a simple TaskChain execution*

The Tasking Live View can be shown in any of the runtime workspaces, meaning that you have to launch the sample launch configuration from the launch configuration view. (See Figure 4-3.) There is again a dedicated launch configuration for this sample.

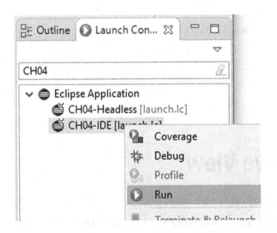

Figure 4-3. *Launch the Chapter 4 sample*

To show the view, I will use a similar launch configuration as already used in Chapter 2. Launch it and open the view by clicking Window ➤ Show View ➤ Other… in the main toolbar and selecting the `Tasking Live View` from there, as shown in Figures 4-4 and 4-5, respectively.

Figure 4-4. *Finding the Tasking Live View in Other…*

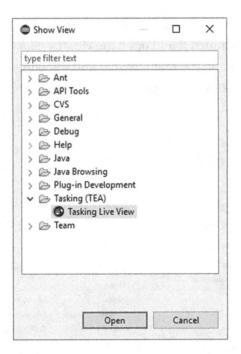

Figure 4-5. *Select Tasking Live View and press Open*

Now run the sample TaskChain in the same way as described in Chapter 2. Find the TaskChain as shown in Figure 4-6. You will see progress reporting in the view and the output shown in Figure 4-7, although the Task from this sample is simply too fast for progress reporting to be of much use in this simple case.

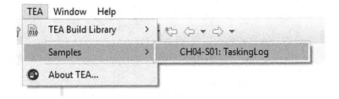

Figure 4-6. *Execute sample TaskChain for TaskingLog*

Figure 4-7. *Sample logging output*

One last thing to note is output coloring. In the IDE Console view, output will be colored depending on the severity of the log method used, as can also be seen in Figure 4-7. To avoid problems with third-party tools capturing output of headless execution, output there will not be colored.

CHAPTER 5

Tasks

A Task is basically a piece of executable code that is dynamically created and managed by TEA. You can use dependency injection (DI) to obtain objects in the DI context of the Task (or any parent context—see Figure 3-4). You can think of it as a more powerful Runnable.

A simple Task implementation looks like the code snippet in Listing 5-1.

Listing 5-1. A Very Simple Task

```
import org.eclipse.e4.core.di.annotations.Execute;
import org.eclipse.tea.core.services.TaskingLog;

public class SampleSimpleTask {
    @Execute
    public void doIt(TaskingLog log) {
        log.info("Hello World");
    }
}
```

Something worth noting here is that the sample Task does not implement an interface. The only requirement for a Task is that it has a single method annotated with @Execute. This method can use DI. Every Task has its own dependency injection context. This is important, for instance, when injecting a TaskProgressTracker, which we will cover in detail in Chapter 8.

Naming

Apart from the required @Execute method, you can influence how TEA handles and presents a Task (in logs, UI, etc.).

Providing a proper name for a Task is the most basic thing you need to do. By default, TEA will use the simple class name of a Task to show in logs and the Tasking Live View (If you revisit any of the samples from Chapter 4, you will see this because we have not named a Task until now. For instance, see Figure 4-7.)

The recommended method of providing a name is to use the @Named annotation. This annotation is usually used in DI to point to a certain named object in the context instead of using the class name as key. In this case it provides the name for the Task, as shown in Listing 5-2.

Listing 5-2. Naming a Task with the @Named annotation

```
@Named("Named Task")
public class TaskStaticNamed {
    @Execute
    public void run(TaskingLog log) {
        log.info("Hello World");
    }
}
```

This Task will be shown as "Named Task" instead of TaskStaticNamed whenever TEA needs to display a Task name—in the log as well as in the Tasking Live View.

The second method of giving a Task a name is to provide a toString method on the object, as seen in Listing 5-3.

Listing 5-3. Naming a Task with the toString Method

```
public class TaskDynamicNamed {

    @Execute
    public void run(TaskingLog log) {
        log.info("Hello World");
    }

    @Override
    public String toString() {
        return "Named " +
            System.currentTimeMillis();
    }

}
```

Both methods have the exact same effect with regards to TEA. However, the first one is preferred because it is more compact to write and it is possible to implement a toString method for different use cases if the annotation is present. The toString method will not be evaluated if the annotation is present. On the other hand, the annotation can only hold a static value. Using toString allows for a more dynamic name (as seen in Listing 5-3). Figure 5-1 shows how both variants look in action.

Figure 5-1. *@Named and toString in Action*

Hint   Run the TEA-Book-Samples launch configuration and find
the TEA ➤ Samples ➤ CH05-S01: Naming entry in the TEA menu.

Incidentally, the same naming logic is also used for TaskChain
implementations.

Return Values

It is not normally possible to return any values from a Task. Since the
framework is always the caller for each Task (as we will describe in Chapter 6,
Tasks are passed to the framework, and the framework is responsible for
executing them at the right point in time), it would not make that much sense
in the first place.

But, to be able to tell the framework how well the Task did, it can
return an IStatus[1] to it, as shown in Listing 5-4.

Listing 5-4. Returning Information from a Task

```
public class TaskRunSomething{
    @Execute
    public IStatus run() {
        return new Status(IStatus.WARNING,
            "org.eclipse.tea.demo",
            "Something smells fishy");
    }
}
```

The Task will be displayed and/or logged with a warning accordingly;
see Figure 5-2. The second way to influence a Task result is by throwing
an OperationCanceledException. Both methods are described in more
detail when we talk about progress reporting in Chapter 8.

---

[1]org.eclipse.core.runtime.IStatus

Figure 5-2. *Returning an IStatus to the TEA framework*

Output Capturing

Sometimes a `Task` needs to call code that is not aware of TEA at all; it could be any preexisting code. In this case, the code may do a plethora of different things to log things, including writing to `System.out` and `System.err`. This will work just fine in headless environments because TEA logs to the same place in these cases. However, when running a `Task` in the IDE, this is suboptimal. Output is partially in the Tasking Console, and the `System.out`/`System.err` part goes to the output streams of the IDE itself. That's definitely what we don't want.

To get around this, TEA provides an annotation (`@TaskCaptureStdOutput`) for `Task` implementations that instructs the framework to redirect `System.out` and `System.err` to the `TaskingLog` for as long as the Task `@Execute` method runs, as seen in Listing 5-5.

Listing 5-5. Capturing Output of Third-party Code

```
@TaskCaptureStdOutput
public class TaskRunSomething{
    private void someExternalStuff() {
        System.err.println("Something hidden");
    }

    @Execute
```

```
public void callExternal() {
        someExternalStuff();
    }
}
```

Figure 5-3 shows how the code in Listing 5-5 will show up in the sample IDE (run TEA ➤ Samples ➤ CH05-S03: Output Capturing).

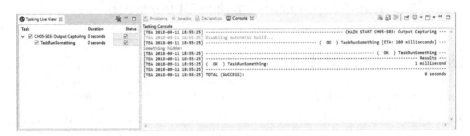

Figure 5-3. *Capturing output from System.err*

CHAPTER 6

TaskChains

The TaskChain is the central concept of TEA. A Task without a TaskChain is only half the fun because it cannot be executed as stand-alone by the TEA Engine. Thus, a TaskChain is required at all times.

To create a new TaskChain, it is necessary to do the following:

1. *Create a class that implements* TaskChain: This class is an empty TEA service interface that is used as a marker only.

2. *Implement a method annotated with the* @TaskChainContextInit *annotation:* This method is called to initialize the list of Task objects/classes that make up the actual TaskChain.

3. *Add a* @Component *annotation:* This step is not strictly required because any TaskChain can be executed manually via the TEA APIs (using org. eclipse.tea.core.TaskingEngine.runTaskChain (TaskExecutionContext)). When the annotation is present, the TaskChain is registered as an OSGi service—as previously described—and can be provided via the TEA UI (the dynamic TEA menu). It is also possible to execute the TaskChain using the headless TEA application without writing any additional code in this case.

© Markus Duft 2018
M. Duft, *Eclipse TEA Revealed*, https://doi.org/10.1007/978-1-4842-4093-9_6

A typical simple TaskChain will always look like the one in Listing 6-1.

Listing 6-1. A Very Simple TaskChain

```
@Component
public class TaskChainRunSomething
                            implements TaskChain {
    @TaskChainContextInit
    public void init(TaskExecutionContext c) {
        c.addTask(TaskRunSomething.class);
    }
}
```

Note   Looking back at the samples in previous chapters, you will notice (when looking at the sample code in the TEA workspace) that all of them have a TaskChain that looks like the one in Listing 6-1.

The init method receives the TaskExecutionContext to initialize with Task objects (which can be specified as Class or instance of the according Class) and adds all of them to it.

If a Task is added as using its Class instead of providing an instance, the TEA framework will instantiate the Class at some point during preparation of TaskChain execution.

Headless vs. UI

In some situations, it might be necessary to react to the fact that a TaskChain is executed in a headless context. This might happen both statically and dynamically. What I mean by this is that, for some TaskChain implementations, it might not make any sense to specify a location in the dynamic TEA menu to display it (meaning it is visible to the user of the IDE, something I will discuss later in this chapter), when it can actually

only run in a headless context. On the other hand, some TaskChain
implementations run fine in both situations but may need to adapt their
behavior. An example would be a TaskChain that sets up a workspace from
scratch in a headless environment, but operates on existing projects in an
existing workspace in a developer's IDE.

To determine whether TEA is running headless, you can use a small
helper method, which is passed the current TaskExecutionContext, as
shown in Listing 6-2.

Listing 6-2. Detecting the Headless Mode

```java
public class TaskChainRunSomething
                        implements TaskChain {
    @TaskChainContextInit
    public void init(TaskExecutionContext c) {
        if(TaskingInjectionHelper
                    .isHeadless(c.getContext())) {
            c.addTask(TaskRunHeadless.class);
        } else {
            c.addTask(TaskRunIDE.class);
        }
    }
}
```

Let's assume that the two Task implementations referenced here
simply output "Hello IDE" and "Hello Headless," respectively. You can
use the CH06-Headless launch configuration from the TEA workspace
to run the headless sample, and TEA ➤ Samples ➤ CH06-S01: Adapt to
Headless from the runtime workspace (use the TEA-Book-Samples launch
configuration) to run the IDE variant. See Figure 6-1 and Figure 6-2 for an
example of how this looks.

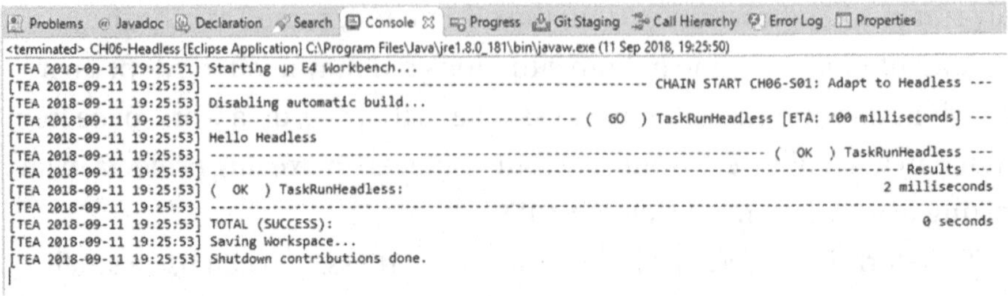

Figure 6-1. *TaskChain in headless mode*

Figure 6-2. *The same TaskChain executed from the runtime workspace*

Note   The `TaskExecutionContext` can be injected nearly everywhere in TEA, not only in `@TaskChainContextInit` methods. For instance, any `Task` or any `TaskingLifecycleListener` method can accept it. This provides a sufficient amount of flexibility to react in certain situations such as to clone a repository and import projects in a headless environment, but not when running the `TaskChain` via the UI.

Using UI to Configure a TaskChain

TEA provides a mechanism that can be used to present UI to configure a TaskChain (when actually run from the UI). This can be achieved by implementing an additional method annotated with @TaskChainUiInit. This method will be called when the TaskChain is launched from the UI, but ignored when run in a headless application. A good example for this is the SamplePreferenceImportTaskChain from the org.eclipse.tea. samples project, as seen in Listing 6-3.

Listing 6-3. Using a UI to Initialize a TaskChain

```
@Component
public class SamplePreferenceImportTaskChain
                          implements TaskChain {

    public static final String KEY =
                          "preferenceFile";
    public static final String FORCE =
                          "forceImport";

    @TaskChainContextInit
    public void init(TaskExecutionContext c,
            @Named(KEY) String filename,
            @Named(FORCE) boolean force) {

        c.addTask(new TaskImportPreferences(
                new File(filename), force));
    }

    @TaskChainUiInit
    public void selectFile(Shell parent,
                          IEclipseContext ctx) {
        FileDialog dlg = new FileDialog(
                          parent, SWT.OPEN);
```

```
            String path = dlg.open();
            if (path == null) {
                    throw new
                            OperationCanceledException();
            }
            ctx.set(FORCE, MessageDialog
                    .openQuestion(parent,
                            "Override preferences",
                            "Override existing non-default
                                    preferences?"));
            ctx.set(KEY, path);

    }

}
```

Note   The selectFile method requests injection of a Shell object. TEA will make sure to inject the proper active Eclipse Workbench Window's Shell when requested by a method with then @TaskChainUiInit annotation.

The @TaskChainUiInit method will be called before the @TaskChainContextInit method so it can set up additional things. In this case, it prompts the user for a filename and stores this information in the IEclipseContext, which is the dependency injection context used to inject the methods of the TaskChain.

In this particular situation, the TaskChain is not able to execute without having the KEY value set in the DI context. This means that the TaskChain can actually not run in a headless environment. We will discuss better and/or different configuration mechanisms in Chapter 7. You can also add @Optional to the @Named(KEY) String filename parameter. This would allow executing even if KEY is not present in the DI context. It will be passed null instead in this case.

Identifying a TaskChain

In both headless and UI environments, there is the need to be able to reference a TaskChain implementation. In headless environments, we want to tell the headless application which TaskChain to execute. In the UI, we want to choose the TaskChain to execute from the dynamic TEA menu.

By default, TEA will use the TaskChain implementations class name for both purposes. The headless application can be passed the fully qualified class name to execute. The TEA menu will use the simple class name (without package) and display this to the user.

This can definitely be improved! TEA provides a few annotations and mechanisms for this purpose, as shown in Listing 6-4.

Listing 6-4. Naming and Describing a TaskChain

```
@TaskChainId(
            description = "CH06-S02: Visibility",
            alias="CH06Visibility")
@TaskChainMenuEntry(
            path = { "Samples", "CH06-Nested" },
            icon="resources/sample.png")
@Component
public class TaskChainRunSomething
                        implements TaskChain {
    @TaskChainContextInit
    public void init(TaskExecutionContext c) {
        c.addTask(TaskRunSomething.class);
    }
}
```

See Figure 6-3 for how this TaskChain would be displayed in the TEA menu.

65

Figure 6-3. *Example for specifying a menu path with*
@TaskChainMenuEntry

Hint   You can see this yourself by running the TEA-Book-Samples
launch configuration from the TEA workspace.

The @TaskChainId and @TaskChainMenuEntry annotations can be
seen very frequently on TaskChain implementations since doing so greatly
improves the presentation and accessibility of them.

The @TaskChainId annotation is mainly used to make identification
of the TaskChain more convenient in different situations. It has three
attributes:

- description: A human readable description of the
  TaskChain. This will be used by the dynamic TEA menu
  to display the TaskChain.

- alias: One or more aliases that can be used to instruct
  the headless application(s) to execute this TaskChain.

- retries: In case any of the Task instances in this
  TaskChain fails, it configures the number of times TEA
  retries execution of the TaskChain as a whole.
  It defaults to 1.

The @TaskChainMenuEntry annotation is used to control the placement of the menu entry corresponding to this TaskChain in the dynamic TEA menu in the main Eclipse toolbar. It has four attributes:

- path: Specifies the menu path as an array of String objects. TEA will create sub-menus as required and specified. Listing 6-4 and Figure 6-3 demonstrate how this works.

- icon: Specifies an icon to use for the menu entry. The path of the icon is relative to the plug-in root that defines the TaskChain. Make sure to include the icon in the plug-ins build.properties (to be found in the root of each plug-in project) as binary include; forgetting this is a common mistake. (See Figure 6-4.)

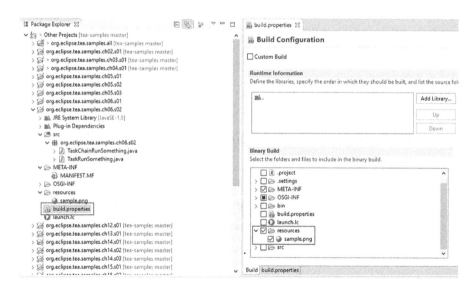

Figure 6-4. *Don't forget to add icons to be included in binary builds*

- **development**: A Boolean value specifying whether the TaskChain is for development purposes only. The effect of this is that the TaskChain will not be shown by default. It will only be visible in the menu when switching on development mode in the settings, as shown in Figure 6-5.

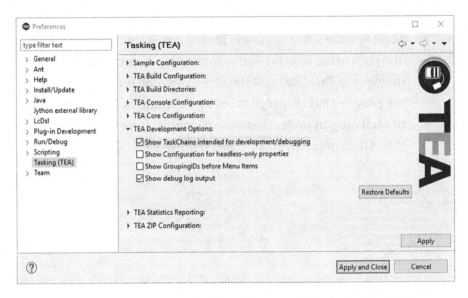

Figure 6-5. *Setting to show development TaskChain in the TEA menu*

- **groupingId**: This is a more advanced possibility to influence how menu entries are sorted and grouped in the menu. Since this process can get quite complex, I will describe this separately.

> **Note**   The dynamic TEA menu usually only displays menu entries
> that relate directly to a `TaskChain`. TEA provides a mechanism to
> hook arbitrary code (even dynamically) to the menu by implementing
> a `TaskingAdditionalMenuEntryProvider`. This components
> `getAdditionalEntries` method is called whenever the menu is
> about to show, so make sure to keep it fast.

Grouping Menu Entries

You have heard about the `groupingId` attribute of the `@TaskChainMenuEntry`
annotation. It can be used to group menu entries, but how does this work?

First, you must implement a `TaskingMenuDecoration` component that
contains the grouping ID definitions, as shown in Listing 6-5.

Listing 6-5. Defining Menu Grouping IDs

```
@Component
public class MyGroupings
            implements TaskingMenuDecoration {

    @TaskingMenuGroupingId(
            beforeGroupingId = NO_GROUPING)
    public static final String GID_A = "my.A";

    @TaskingMenuGroupingId(
            afterGroupingId = GID_A)
    public static final String GID_B = "my.B";
}
```

Briefly explained, the first (GID_A) grouping will move all menu entries with this groupingId to before any menu entries without any groupingId set. The second (GID_B) grouping will move any menu entry with that groupingId to after any menu entry with groupingId GID_A. This means that entries with groupingId GID_B will end up in between entries with GID_A and entries without any groupingId.

To fully understand this, read more on grouping in Chapter 15.

Styling Sub-Menus

As you saw in Figure 6-3, the sub-menus (CH06-Nested in the picture) do not have any icon. If you want to style a sub-menu with an icon, implement an according TaskingMenuDecoration component. These components can provide static fields with @TaskingMenuPathDecoration annotations, as seen in Listing 6-6.

Listing 6-6. Styling a Sub-Menu

```
@Component
public class MyDeco implements TaskingMenuDecoration {
    @TaskingMenuPathDecoration(
            menuPath = { "Samples", "CH06-Nested" })
    public static final String SAMPLE_ICON =
                            "resources/sample.png";
}
```

Applied to the previous sample, the menu will change like the one shown in Figure 6-6. Note the additional icon on the sub-menu.

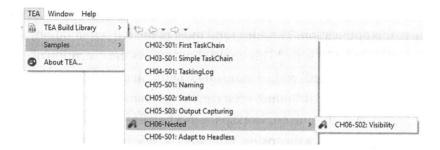

Figure 6-6. *Styled sub-menu with full-menu path*

Note   The styling is applied to the exact matching menu path— to the CH06-Nested item in the sample.

The MyDeco.java in the provided sample projects (org.eclipse. tea.samples.ch06.s02 in this case) has some commented out code so that the icon is not present from the start. Uncomment the code to make the icon appear.

XVFB and Friends

We have talked about headless, but what exactly do we mean by "headless"? It is kind of a gray zone. Headless typically means running on systems without UI. But does that mean that UI code cannot be executed, or that it simply does not display anything? Well, it depends. TEA provides two headless applications under the hood. One is a simple Eclipse IApplication, which can be used to actually run completely headless. UI code will not work when using this application[1] simply because the UI parts of the Eclipse framework are not started at all by this application. On the other hand, there is a second IApplication,

---

[1] org.eclipse.tea.core.internal.TaskingEngineApplication

71

together with a RCP product[2] definition, which binds a headless rendering engine to this application. This idea (and most of the implementation) is taken from the E4 UI tests.[3] This application[4] allows the execution of virtually any UI (-related) code. For instance launching (and debugging) in Eclipse is usually very UI-bound, yet it can be very handy to run a launch configuration from the current workspace in a headless environment.

This, of course, has a downside. Running UI code (typically SWT) will require that UI is accessible. On X11-based systems, this will require a UI to be present. We frequently set up headless Linux systems running Jenkins builds using TEA. All of them have the Jenkins Xvfb plug-in (`https://wiki.jenkins.io/display/JENKINS/Xvfb+Plugin`) installed to make sure an X11 server is available. Nothing is actually ever displayed there (if all goes well); it is just required to be able to initialize and run UI code.

Updates

In my opinion, the only major downside of TEA in headless environments is updates. When installing Eclipse on servers, somebody needs to make updates from time to time, and at least once required TEA component implementation changes.

At the company I work for, we have solved this problem by implementing an automatic update as `TaskingHeadlessLifeCycle`. Eclipse will check for (and apply) updates on every startup. The mechanism is unfortunately relying on third-party software as of now (so it cannot be added to TEA directly), but it is definitely feasible to implement if done in an environment-specific fashion without too much effort.

---

[2]`https://help.eclipse.org/photon/topic/org.eclipse.pde.doc.user/guide/tools/editors/product_editor/configuration.htm`

[3]`https://github.com/eclipse/eclipse.platform.ui/blob/master/tests/org.eclipse.e4.ui.tests/src/org/eclipse/e4/ui/tests/application/HeadlessContextPresentationEngine.java`

[4]`org.eclipse.tea.core.ui.internal.TaskingEngineExtendedApplication`

Configuration

Another difference between headless and UI is the way configuration values can be set and/or passed to TEA. In UI, TEA provides a dynamic preference page implementation, allowing users to manually configure settings. On the command line, this is not very handy. Thus, it is possible to set any configuration value (you will learn how to create your own configuration in Chapter 7) from a property file. This property file may look something like Listing 6-7.

Listing 6-7. A Sample headless.properties File

```
measureMemoryUsage = true
showDebugLogs = false
compileRetries = 3
```

This property file can be passed to the headless application using the -properties <file> argument. It can reside anywhere on disc; there is no association to any Eclipse workspace and/or project.

Each line in the property file sets a value of a field defined in a TaskingConfigurationExtension implementation—more on this in Chapter 7.

In the IDE, each TEA configuration option is accessible through Window ➤ Preferences ➤ Tasking (TEA). You can have a look at it now, but we'll cover all of this (you may have guessed it) in Chapter 7.

Life Cycle

Apart from implementing TaskChain components, TEA also supports hooking on the life cycle of them. This can be used to implement TaskChain- or Task-overarching features. TEA itself uses this feature to implement most additional logging, status handling, statistic handling, and other features. A simple TaskingLifeCycleListener looks similar to the example in Listing 6-8.

Listing 6-8. A Simple TaskingLifeCycleListener

```
@Component
public class Listener
            implements TaskingLifeCycleListener {
      @BeginTaskChain
      public void chainBegin(TaskingLog log) {
            log.info("beginning...");
      }
}
```

The listener in Listing 6-8 again uses the OSGi DS @Component annotation to register the service with the runtime. Once it is registered (that is, when the bundle was loaded and started by the runtime), it will be called whenever a TaskChain execution is about to begin.

There are different situations a life cycle handler can react to. A single listener may hook on all available life cycle events, as each of them is hooked on by providing a method with a dedicated per-event annotation:

- @CreateContext: Called when a new TaskExecutionContext is created, right after the context has been initialized from the TaskChain implementation by calling the @TaskChainContextInit method.

- @DisposeContext: Called after execution of a context has finished, right before the context is removed.

- @BeginTaskChain: Called right before a TaskChain execution starts (in other words, the first Task is executed).

- @FinishTaskChain: Called after the last Task has finished executing (or execution aborted with an error). The state of the TaskChain can be determined by injecting and examining a MultiStatus object.

- @BeginTask: Called before execution of an individual Task. The actual Task object can be accessed by injecting @Named(TaskingInjectionHelper.CTX_TASK) Object task as parameter into the method.

- @FinishTask: Called after execution of an individual Task has finished. Injection is performed using the Task injection context, so an IStatus object can be injected and examined to determine the Task state.

A quite complete example of how to implement a TaskingLifecycleListener can be found in org.eclipse.tea.core. internal.listeners.TaskingStatusTracker. It reacts to nearly all of those events to keep track of TaskChain and Task execution and state. This information is then used indirectly, for instance, in the Tasking Live View to display state to the user. Figure 6-7 hightlights the parts of the output that are produced by the TaskingStatusTracker, demonstrated with a previous sample. As you can see, most of the output is actually done by this component.

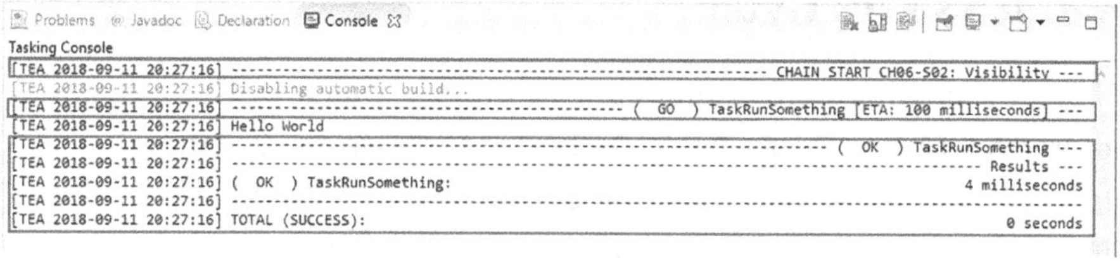

Figure 6-7. *Output produced by TaskingStatusTracker*

Finally, The @TaskingLifeCyclePriority annotation provides a way to control order of execution of life cycle handlers since this can be important in some scenarios—for instance if access to a UI component is required in one listener and the UI is initialized by another listener. The first one will fail if not executed after the second one has initialized the UI. The default priority is 10. The higher the priority, the earlier (at startup) the life cycle listener implementation will be executed. The order of contributions on shutdown is the reverse startup order. Something you want to execute very early would look like the code in Listing 6-9.

Listing 6-9. Defining the Priority of a TaskingLifeCycleListener

```
@Component
@TaskingLifeCyclePriority(200)
public class Listener
        implements TaskingLifeCycleListener {...}
```

TEA built-in listeners use priorities between 10 and 100.

Headless Life Cycle

In headless environments, additional life cycle is available. This is mostly required for TEA internals, but it can be used to have an even more outermost bracket around your TaskChain. The most notable difference between the normal TaskingLifecycleListener and the TaskingHeadlessLifeCycle is that it can influence startup of the headless application, as demonstrated in Listing 6-10.

Listing 6-10. A Sample TaskingHeadlessLifeCycle

```
@Component
public class TestHeadlessLifecycle
            implements TaskingHeadlessLifeCycle {
```

```
@HeadlessStartup
public StartupAction start(TaskingLog log) {
        log.debug("Startup...");

        if(Boolean.getBoolean("restart")) {
                log.debug("Restarting...");
                return StartupAction.RESTART;
        }

        return StartupAction.CONTINUE;
}

@HeadlessShutdown
public void stop(TaskingLog log)
                throws Exception {
        log.debug("Shutdown...");
    }
}
```

Note   The @HeadlessStatup method must return a value of the StartupAction enumeration. It has two possible values: CONTINUE and RESTART.

Returning StartupAction.RESTART from the @HeadlessStartup method can be used to implement automatic updating of the Eclipse running TEA in headless mode: (check for and apply updates and return RESTART on success).

You can run the sample in Listing 6-10 by running the CH06-Lifecycle launch configuration from the TEA workspace. You will notice that TEA will be stuck in a restart loop, as shown in Figure 6-8.

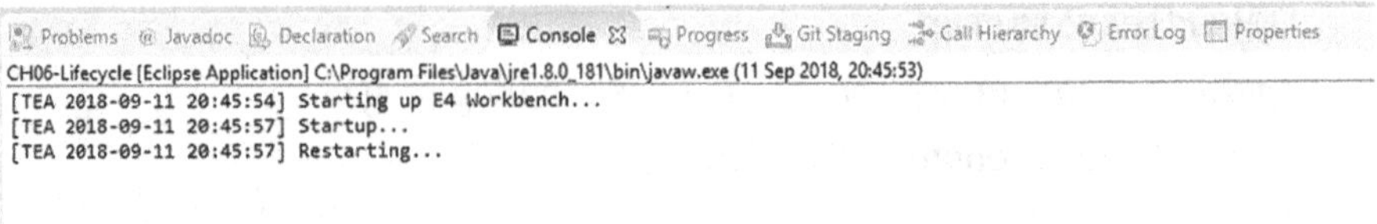

```
[Problems] [Javadoc] [Declaration] [Search] [Console] [Progress] [Git Staging] [Call Hierarchy] [Error Log] [Properties]
CH06-Lifecycle [Eclipse Application] C:\Program Files\Java\jre1.8.0_181\bin\javaw.exe (11 Sep 2018, 20:45:53)
[TEA 2018-09-11 20:45:54] Starting up E4 Workbench...
[TEA 2018-09-11 20:45:57] Startup...
[TEA 2018-09-11 20:45:57] Restarting...
```

Figure 6-8. *Restart loop*

You can "fix" the issue by removing the line highlighted in Figure 6-9 from the `launch.lc` file in the `org.eclipse.tea.samples.ch06.s03` project.

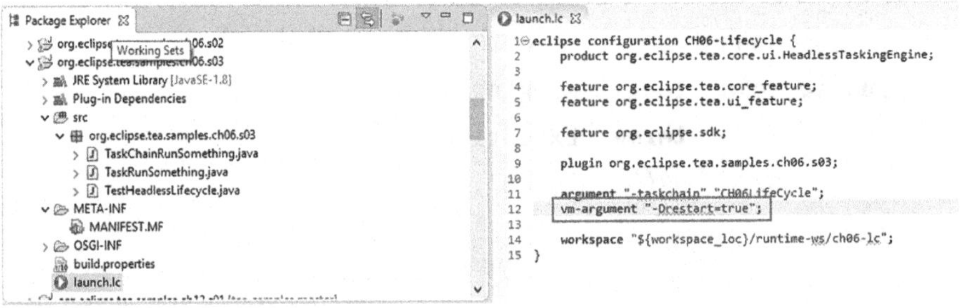

Figure 6-9. *Remove -Drestart=true to stop TEA from looping*

Now re-running the same launch configuration from the `Launch Configuration View` will result in a smoothly running application.

CHAPTER 7

Configuration

In this chapter, we will take a close look at how to provide configuration to TaskChain and Task objects.

TEA allows custom components to implement services of type TaskingConfigurationExtension. You can provide new and additional configuration options to TEA using plain Java fields in these services. TaskingConfigurationExtension is special in a certain way: TEA will create new instances of these services whenever applying configuration to the system, regardless of the OSGi service type (which allows—and defaults to—reusing service instances). This is necessary since there are different configuration sources (headless.properties, Eclipse preferences) that can lead to different configuration values.

TEA itself uses the same mechanism to expose its built-in configuration options. A typical user-provided configuration extension looks like the one in Listing 7-1.

Listing 7-1. A Sample TaskingConfigurationExtension

```
@TaskingConfig(description = "CH07 Configuration")
@Component
public class SimpleConfig
        implements TaskingConfigurationExtension {
    @TaskingConfigProperty(
            description = "My String")
    public String myString = "default";
}
```

© Markus Duft 2018
M. Duft, *Eclipse TEA Revealed*, https://doi.org/10.1007/978-1-4842-4093-9_7

Again, custom implementations are registered using the OSGi DS
@Component annotation.

There are multiple things worth noting in the previous code sample:

- The @TaskingConfig annotation provides a human-
  readable description of the configuration object as
  a whole. This description is used when creating the
  dynamic Eclipse Preferences page, which holds all
  configurations contributed to TEA. You can see an
  example in Figure 7-1.

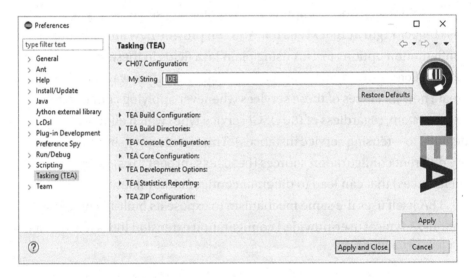

Figure 7-1. *Simple configuration in TEA preference page*

- The @TaskingConfigProperty annotation marks a non-
  static field in the implementation class that should
  be used as the configuration value. The description
  property of the annotation will again be used to
  present the property on the preference page. Again,
  see Figure 7-1. There are two more properties on the
  annotation not shown here: name and headlessOnly.

The name can be used to provide an alternative name for the property when set through a property file for the headless application. This can use characters not otherwise valid for Java field names—for instance, a dot. The headlessOnly property will simply hide a configuration option from the generated preference page because it is intended to be set by a property file in headless mode only.

- The actual field which is defined in the class. Its name is the default name of the property for definition in a property file for headless applications (unless overridden using the @TaskingConfigProperty' name attribute). It can be assigned a value, which is the default value for the property if neither a property file (headless) nor a preference setting (UI) exists.

Note   The name of property fields must be globally unique among all TaskingConfigurationExtension implementations since their plain field names are used in headless.properties files! TEA will verify that fields are unique on configuration initialization for you and log warnings to the TaskingLog.

The preference page (unlike other Eclipse preference pages) provides a Restore Defaults button for each sub-section (directly relating to a single TaskingConfigurationExtension). This button will not affect any of the other sub-sections, so individual settings can be reverted to defaults without affecting other TaskingConfigurationExtensions.

Configuration objects are discovered and initialized early during TEA Engine startup. This means that all custom components can have all configuration objects injected. Listing 7-2 shows how this is done.

Listing 7-2. Consuming Configuration in a Task

```
public class TaskRunSomething {
    @Execute
    public void run(TaskingLog log,
                      SimpleConfig config) {
        log.info("Hello " + config.myString);
    }
}
```

This `Task` will accept a `SimpleConfig` object. This object has been instantiated and filled with configuration values as appropriate by the current mode of operation. Values can be read by simply accessing the field; writes will not be persistent.

Note   It is possible to add methods (and also fields without annotations) to `TaskingConfigurationExtension` implementations. This can be used to provide complex getters backed by configuration values set using the TEA configuration mechanism.

Let's now put everything together and try it out. Run the TEA-Book-Samples launch configuration from the TEA workspace to launch a runtime workspace and go to Window ➤ Preferences ➤ Tasking (TEA) to see the preference page shown in Figure 7-1. Try putting a different value than the default ("default"). Now run the `TaskChain` from TEA ➤ Samples ➤ CH07-S01: Simple Config to see the output shown in Figure 7-2.

```
[TEA 2018-09-12 07:53:03] ------------------------------------------------- CHAIN START CH07-S01: Simple Config ---
[TEA 2018-09-12 07:53:03] Disabling automatic build...
[TEA 2018-09-12 07:53:03] --------------------------------------- (  GO  ) TaskRunSomething [ETA: 100 milliseconds] ---
[TEA 2018-09-12 07:53:03] Hello IDE!
[TEA 2018-09-12 07:53:03] ------------------------------------------------------------------- (  OK  ) TaskRunSomething ---
[TEA 2018-09-12 07:53:03] -------------------------------------------------------------------------------------- Results ---
[TEA 2018-09-12 07:53:03] (  OK  ) TaskRunSomething:                                                        2 milliseconds
[TEA 2018-09-12 07:53:03] -------------------------------------------------------------------------------------------------
[TEA 2018-09-12 07:53:03] TOTAL (SUCCESS):                                                                      0 seconds
```

Figure 7-2. *Configure via Eclipse preferences*

You can run the CH07-Config launch configuration to see the result output in headless mode. Figure 7-3 shows the output as well as the headless.properties configuration files. The output is located in the org.eclipse.tea.samples.ch07.s01 project.

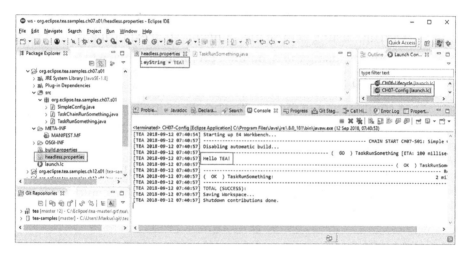

Figure 7-3. *Using headless.properties to configure TEA*

Configuration Sources

TEA will fetch values from different sources, depending on the mode of operation. All of them are abstracted by the TaskingConfigurationStore interface. This interface is special for TEA, because it is not special. This is one of the very few interfaces that is actually just an interface.

TEA does not use OSGi to discover implementations. When creating a
TaskingEngine programmatically, the TaskingEngine.withConfigur
ation(TaskingConfigurationStore) method can be used to provide
alternative implementations if required. Otherwise one of the three
implementations is picked as appropriate:

- PropertyConfigurationStore: A simple store that is
  backed by a property file passed to the headless TEA
  application(s). This mechanism is not used anywhere
  in the IDE, only in headless mode.

- TaskingEclipsePreferenceStore: A store backed by
  Eclipse preferences. The scope of all preferences is the
  TEA plug-in itself. Preferences can be manipulated
  with all existing Eclipse mechanisms, such exporting,
  importing, using the dynamic TEA preference page to
  manually configure, and so on.

- A combination of the two: The headless application
  with UI support (discussed previous) will use
  a combination of both stores. It will query the
  PropertyConfigurationStore first, and then fall back to
  the TaskingEclipsePreferenceStore if no value could
  be found.

Runtime Configuration Updates

You may run into the situation where a Task updates Eclipse preferences
and, hence, relevant configuration for the next Task. One example for
such a situation is a Task setting up a workspace from scratch. At some
point, it might import projects containing .epf preference files and

import those as well. Without additional magic, this will not be taken into account by any following Task because the initialization of configuration usually only happens once. Luckily, TEA can help us out using the @TaskReloadConfiguration annotation, as shown in Listing 7-3.

Listing 7-3. Reloading Configuration after Execution of a Task

```
@TaskReloadConfiguration
public class SomeTask {
    @Execute
    public void import() {
        // import preferences
    }
}
```

This code will instruct TEA to reload the configuration once this Task has finished before moving on to the next Task.

I'm aware that this situation is somewhat hypothetical. For a concrete (but large) example, take a look at TaskImportPreferences[1]—it does this exact thing.

Note   TEA eats its own dog food to implement this feature. There is a class ConfigurationRefresher,[2] which is a TaskingLifeCycleListener. It reacts on @FinishTask for any Task with the @TaskReloadConfiguration annotation to reinitialize the configuration.

---

[1]org.eclipse.tea.library.build.tasks.TaskImportPreferences
[2]org.eclipse.tea.core.internal.listeners.ConfigurationRefresher

CHAPTER 8

Progress Reporting

A whole lot of work is only half the fun for the one watching it being done. Thus, it would make sense to inform those watching about the progress of lengthy operations. Whoever has dealt with progress reporting before knows it can be hard sometimes, especially when reporting progress spanning several operations with different runtime durations.

TEA tries to take away most of the pain from progress reporting. Traditionally, there are two different kinds of progress calculation: either the operation itself reports how far down the road it already went or somebody external to the operation monitors and estimates progress based on historic data. TEA does both. And it can mix and match both. Because why not?

Every Task in TEA has full control over its progress reporting and how it is done. TEA combines all the setups at TaskChain level and calculates total and individual progress. Let's have a closer look at the two different methods of dealing with this topic.

The Manual Way

TEA uses a system similar to Eclipse' IProgressMonitor. (In fact, it uses this infrastructure under the hood as well.) This means that, initially, a number of "ticks" are collected, which is an abstraction of a certain amount of work. This allows putting different Task objects in relation with regards to their "size" (execution duration). During execution, the amount of processed ticks is increased—in this case, manually by the Task whenever work is done, as shown in Listing 8-1.

© Markus Duft 2018
M. Duft, *Eclipse TEA Revealed*, https://doi.org/10.1007/978-1-4842-4093-9_8

Listing 8-1. Manual Progress Reporting

```java
public class TaskRunSomething {
    private int work = 10;

    @Execute
    public void work(
            TaskingLog log,
            TaskProgressTracker tracker) {

        for(int i = 0; i < work; ++i) {
            tracker.worked(1);
            log.info("worked");
            Thread.sleep(100);
        }

        log.info("done");
    }

    @TaskProgressProvider
    public int getAmount() {
        return work;
    }
}
```

This sample shows how to do it fully manually:

1. The Task initializes its work amount in the getAmount method. This method is used as provider for work amount by TEA due to the presence of the @TaskProgressProvider annotation.

2. The Task requests injection of its TaskProgressTracker. This is a per-Task object that allows updating the current work amount. It also allows checking for cancelation (isCanceled)

and setting a sub-task name (setTaskName—this
may or may not be displayed in progress reporting,
depending on the way and location where progress
is visualized).

3. The Task updates the already processed amount
    of work periodically, whenever work actually
    happened. The Task should take care of not
    reporting more work done as initially estimated.
    TEA will not reject such updates, but more than
    100% progress is not displayed and is discarded.

When executed (again, use the TEA-Book-Samples launch
configuration) via TEA ➤ Samples ➤ CH08-S01: Progress Tracking, you
will notice that the execution takes a little while. The progress in Eclipse
Progress View, as well as in the Tasking Live View, will be updated
whenever the worked method is called. This is shown in Figure 8-1.

Figure 8-1. *Visibility of progress reporting in TEA*

Note   The worked method on the `TaskProgressTracker` accepts an integer, which means you can report more than one unit of work ("tick") as done. This can be handy, for instance, when estimating 10 ticks for processing a single "whatever" and later on skipping one of three "whatevers". In this case, make sure to call `worked(10)`, so that the skipped "whatever" is accounted for in the progress reporting. Cancelation and work ticks work in a very similar way to the Eclipse `IProgressMonitor` interface. There is plenty of documentation on that[1], so you can also get some ideas from there.

The TaskProgressEstimationService

The simplest way to deal with progress reporting is not to care at all. In this case, TEA will query the OSGi runtime for a `TaskProgressEstimationService`. TEA has a sane default implementation of this service, so usually there'll be no need to replace it (but it is possible if you get OSGi to rank your service implementation higher).

This service will be notified when a `Task` starts and when it stops. It is then responsible for storing this information until later. When the same `Task` is run again, the service will provide an estimation of the amount of work this `Task` will take up.

Now TEA will start "ticking" progress at a fixed rate. This allows for a smoother progress reporting compared to full manual updating or progress.

Estimations are updated on subsequent `Task` executions. If the new execution time is substantially different from the old one (much longer or much shorter), it will replace the stored value. If it is somewhat within the same range, it will update the value by using this formula: `estimation = (old + new) / 2`.

---

[1]`www.eclipse.org/articles/Article-Progress-Monitors/article.html`

> **Note**   A Task can still have a TaskProgressMonitor injected
> with automatic progress reporting. It can be used to check for
> cancelation in this case.

Task Cancelation and State

Task cancelation is closely bound to progress reporting for a reason.
Usually, when displaying progress of an operation in a UI, a cancel button
will be displayed close to it (if cancelation is supported). TEA will always
enable cancelation support when reporting progress upstream (for
example, to Eclipse IProgressMonitor).

Any Task (with either manual or automatic progress reporting) can
have a TaskProgressTracker injected. Listing 8-2 shows how this can be
used to check for cancelation and reacting accordingly.

Listing 8-2. A Cancelable Task

```
public class TaskRunSomething {
    @Execute
    public void cancelable(TaskingLog log,
                TaskProgressTracker tracker)
                throws Exception {
        Thread.sleep(5000);

        if (tracker.isCanceled())
            throw new
                OperationCanceledException();

        log.info("Not canceled!");
    }
}
```

This sample is a good one for both automatic progress reporting as well as cancelation.

1. The Task will have automatic progress estimation and reporting (since it does not say otherwise by having a method with the @TaskProgressProvider annotation, as demonstrated in Listing 8-1).

2. The Task nevertheless requests a TaskProgressTracker and uses it to detect whether the Task has been canceled.

3. In case somebody pressed the cancel button during the five-second sleep call, an OperationCanceledException is thrown. This exception is treated specially and the Task will be assigned the state org.eclipse.core.runtime. Status.CANCEL_STATUS.

When run first, TEA will use a default estimation when calculating the expected duration. This is shown in Figure 8-2 (run TEA ➤ Samples ➤ CH08-S02: Progress Estimation / Cancelation to follow along).

Figure 8-2. *Default estimation for estimated Tasks*

When run once more, you will notice that the estimation has been updated. (The estimation is only updated on *successful* execution of a Task.) Figure 8-3 illustrates this.

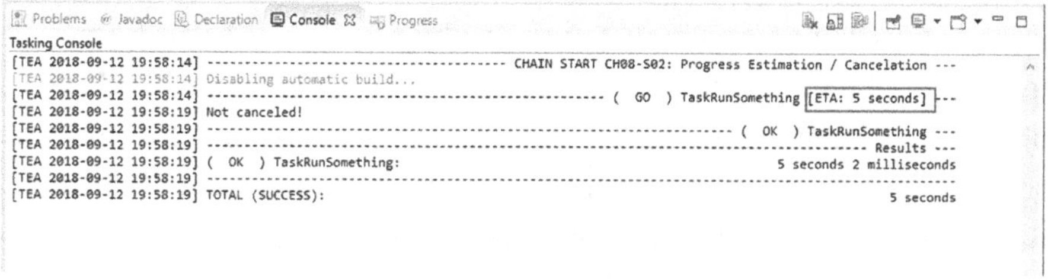

Figure 8-3. *Updated Task runtime estimation*

Finally, Figure 8-4 shows how to cancel a TaskChain, and Figure 8-5 demonstrates what the output of the code from Listing 8-2 looks like in that case.

Figure 8-4. *Canceling a Task from the Progress View*

Figure 8-5. *Canceled Task in Tasking Live View and Console View*

TEA re-uses Eclipse's IStatus and Status objects. Every Task has an associated state. All Task states are then accumulated in a single MultiStatus for the TaskExecutionContext (which corresponds to the state of executing a single TaskChain).

93

TaskingLifeCycleListener implementations can consume these
states by requesting injection of a MultiStatus in @FinishTaskChain
methods or IStatus in @FinishTask methods.

A single Task can influence its state in two distinct ways. The first (and
recommended) one is to simply return an object of type IStatus from
the @Execute method. The second one is to request injection of the Task
objects own DI context and set the state directly (See Listing 8-3). This can
come in handy if a @Execute method is also used in other places (outside
TEA), and, consequently, should have a more specific return value.

Listing 8-3. Setting the Task Status through the IEclipseContext

```
public class TaskRunSomething {
    @Execute
    public void withStatus(IEclipseContext ctx)
                                    throws Exception {
        ctx.set(IStatus.class, new Status(
                IStatus.WARNING,
                "org.eclipse.tea.samples.ch08.s03",
                "Some warning"));
    }
}
```

Take a look at Figure 8-6 to see how the Tasking Live View will render
such a result.

Note   Returning IStatus (or MultiStatus) objects will have the
exact same effect as setting them on an injected IEclipseContext.

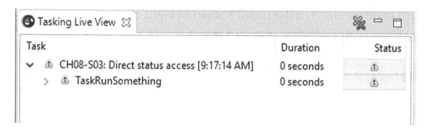

Figure 8-6. *Tasking Live View showing a Task with warning*

Another possibility for Task implementations doing a lot of work, and thus wanting to report a lot of state, is to return/set a MultiStatus object, as seen in Listing 8-4.

Listing 8-4. A Task with Multiple Warnings

```
public class TaskRunSomething {

    @Execute
    public IStatus withStatus() throws Exception {
        MultiStatus ms = new MultiStatus(
                "org.eclipse.tea.samples.s08.s04",
                0, "OK", null);

        ms.add(new Status(IStatus.WARNING,
                "org.eclipse.tea.samples.s08.s04",
                "First warning"));
        ms.add(new Status(IStatus.WARNING,
                "org.eclipse.tea.samples.s08.s04",
                "Second warning"));

        return ms;
    }

}
```

This code will lead to the result shown in Figure 8-7. As you can see, the Task has both warnings attached to it.

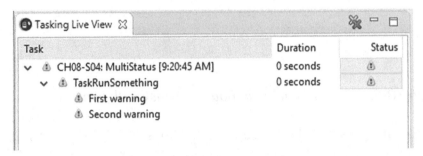

Figure 8-7. *Tasking Live View showing a Task with multiple results (MultiStatus)*

Headless/Console State Handling

The Tasking Live View is nice, especially when it comes to state visualization. How would one get hold of the state of a Task when running headless?

TEA ships with a `TaskingLifeCycleListener` implementation (called `LifecycleAnnouncer`). This listener watches everything that happens in TEA and reports it to the console—you don't need to register it explicitly. This will produce the output shown in Figure 8-8. You have seen similar output since the first sample in the book.

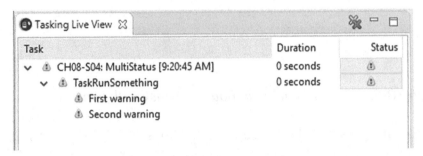

Figure 8-8. *Task states as reported by the TaskingLifeCycleListener*

As you can see, the information is not as excessive as in the Tasking Live View. TEA does not ship with a method to report more details; however, this can be implemented if required very quickly.

CHAPTER 9

Statistics

Experience has shown that (at least in large corporate environments) statistics about `TaskChain` execution can be extremely handy when looking for issues—or when looking for evidence for every developer's the-IDE-is-sooo-slow-again rant. TEA includes a smallish built-in statistics support. It's basically a `TaskingLifeCycleListener` that posts statistics (if enabled) on `@FinishTaskChain` to a configured URL.

Statistics also come in very handy when trying to compare different OS's performance regarding certain operations.

Enabling Statistics Reporting

Figure 9-1 shows how to enable statistics reporting. When configured, the target URL will receive a `POST` request by TEA whenever a `TaskChain` finishes execution. This makes it easy to back the mechanism with any web service (like, for instance, a document-oriented database).

© Markus Duft 2018
M. Duft, *Eclipse TEA Revealed*, https://doi.org/10.1007/978-1-4842-4093-9_9

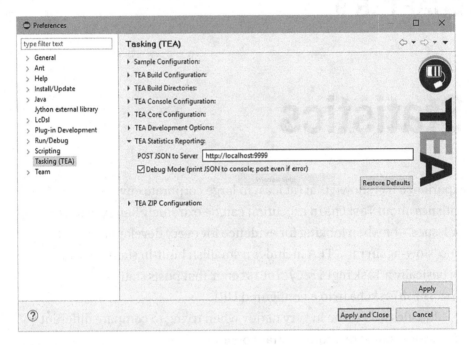

Figure 9-1. *Configure TEA statistics reporting*

Note Enabling the Debug Mode will print the data posted to the server to the TaskingLog as well. If you want to play with it, configure a dummy URL or leave the field empty and check the Debug Mode checkbox, just like in the screenshot. TEA will warn you about not being able to connect (see Figure 9-2); however, you can safely ignore this warning.

Default and Custom Statistics

Running any TaskChain (just pick any from the previous samples in the runtime workspace of the TEA-Book-Samples launch configuration) now will output the statistics JSON after the TaskChain finishes. Figure 9-2 shows how this looks.

```
[R] Problems  @ Javadoc  [R] Declaration  [Q] Console  ⊠  [Q] Progress
Tasking Console
[TEA 2018-09-16 18:33:11] ------------------------------------------------------------- CHAIN START CH08-S04: MultiStatus ---
[TEA 2018-09-16 18:33:11] Disabling automatic build...
[TEA 2018-09-16 18:33:11] -------------------------------------------------- (  GO  ) TaskRunSomething [ETA: 100 milliseconds] ---
[TEA 2018-09-16 18:33:11] -------------------------------------------------------------------- ( WARN ) TaskRunSomething ---
[TEA 2018-09-16 18:33:11] ------------------------------------------------------------------------------------ Results ---
[TEA 2018-09-16 18:33:11] ( WARN ) TaskRunSomething:
[TEA 2018-09-16 18:33:11] --------------------------------------------------------------------------------------------------
[TEA 2018-09-16 18:33:11] TOTAL (SUCCESS):                                                                       0 seconds
[TEA 2018-09-16 18:33:11] will post to server (debug mode enabled):
[TEA 2018-09-16 18:33:11] {
  "timestamp": 1537115591012,
  "taskChainClass": "org.eclipse.tea.samples.ch08.s04.TaskChainRunSomething",
  "taskChainName": "CH08-S04: MultiStatus",
  "duration": 4,
  "tasks": [
    {
      "taskClass": "org.eclipse.tea.samples.ch08.s04.TaskRunSomething",
      "taskName": "TaskRunSomething",
      "status": {
        "severity": 2,
        "message": "OK"
      },
      "duration": 0
    }
  ],
  "sysInfo": {
    "os": "Windows 10:amd64:10.0",
    "processCpuTime": 18500000000,
    "systemLoad": 1.0,
    "processLoad": 0.0,
    "totalSwap": 19685990592,
    "freeSwap": 10286243840,
    "freeMem": 11050156032,
    "totalMem": 17135861760,
    "loadavg": -1.0,
    "processors": 12
  },
  "contributions": {}
}
[TEA 2018-09-16 18:33:11] failed to post statistics: java.net.MalformedURLException
```

Figure 9-2. *Statistics JSON debug output with warning about post failure*

As you can see, the JSON will contain information about the TaskChain, all Task objects, durations, and status (even nested and multistates as described in Chapter 8). It also contains some (nonpersonal, of course) information about the machine that the execution happened on—mainly OS, CPU count, memory information, and load information if available.

Maybe you have also noticed the empty contributions object. This is used for custom contributions to the statistics. This extension mechanism can be used to contribute additional information about the environment (or the specific TaskChain, setup, etc.) For instance, it might be relevant to know how many projects are in a workspace to be able to compare build times between two different machines. If one only has 10 projects, but the other one has 100, it might be arguable that the first one is faster executing the same TaskChain on the workspace. A Task like compiling all projects in the workspace will definitely scale with the amount of projects.

Listing 9-1 shows a simple statistics contribution that will add information about the temperature. As you can see, the contribution is a @Component, as always. It implements TaskingStatisticsContribution as marker interface and has a @TaskingStatisticProvider annotated method. This method must return any object that is serializable to JSON. The object is passed as is to a GSON[1] JSON object mapper

Listing 9-1. Custom Statistics Contribution

```
@Component
public class WeatherContribution implements
TaskingStatisticsContribution {

        @TaskingStatisticProvider(
                            qualifier = "weather")
        public Map<String, Object> getWeather() {
                Map<String, Object> r = new TreeMap<>();
```

---

[1]https://github.com/google/gson

```
        Map<String, String> t = new TreeMap<>();
        t.put("celsius", "34");
        t.put("fahrenh", "93");

        r.put("temps", t);
        r.put("hot", "true");
        return r;
    }
}.
```

Figure 9-3 shows how the JSON changes with the sample code. It will now include the temperature objects as defined in the code.

```
 Problems  @ Javadoc  Declaration  Console 23  Progress
Tasking Console
[TEA 2018-09-16 18:55:06] ----------------------------------------------------------- CHAIN START CH09-S01: Statistics ---
[TEA 2018-09-16 18:55:06] Disabling automatic build...
[TEA 2018-09-16 18:55:06] ----------------------------------------------- (  GO  ) TaskRunSomething [ETA: 100 milliseconds] ---
[TEA 2018-09-16 18:55:06] Hello Statistics!
[TEA 2018-09-16 18:55:06] ---------------------------------------------------------- (  OK  ) TaskRunSomething ---
[TEA 2018-09-16 18:55:06] ---------------------------------------------------------------------------------- Results ---
[TEA 2018-09-16 18:55:06] (  OK  ) TaskRunSomething:                                              1 millisecond
[TEA 2018-09-16 18:55:06] --------------------------------------------------------------------------------------------
[TEA 2018-09-16 18:55:06] TOTAL (SUCCESS):                                                          0 seconds
[TEA 2018-09-16 18:55:06] will post to server (debug mode enabled):
[TEA 2018-09-16 18:55:06] {
  "timestamp": 1537116906773,
  "taskChainClass": "org.eclipse.tea.samples.ch09.s01.TaskChainRunSomething",
  "taskChainName": "CH09-S01: Statistics",
  "duration": 4,
  "tasks": [
    {
      "taskClass": "org.eclipse.tea.samples.ch09.s01.TaskRunSomething",
      "taskName": "TaskRunSomething",
      "status": {
        "severity": 0,
        "message": "Task: TaskRunSomething"
      },
      "duration": 1
    }
  ],
  "sysInfo": {
    "os": "Windows 10:amd64:10.0",
    "processCpuTime": 14687500000,
    "systemLoad": 0.045733649865508035,
    "processLoad": 0.002453284450942514,
    "totalSwap": 19685998592,
    "freeSwap": 10150522880,
    "freeMem": 10862518272,
    "totalMem": 17135861760,
    "loadavg": -1.0,
    "processors": 12
  },
  "contributions": {
    "weather": {
      "hot": "true",
      "temps": {
        "celsius": "34",
        "fahrenh": "93"
      }
    }
  }
}
[TEA 2018-09-16 18:55:06] failed to post statistics: java.net.MalformedURLException
```

Figure 9-3. *Custom statistics contribution in action*

You can see that the information is included in the `contributions` object. This makes it easy to access this information on the target system. Remember that TEA simply performs a `POST` request to the configured URL, so virtually any remote system can be used (NoSQL databases, a custom service, etc.). It just needs to accept JSON input at the specified URL.

To play with this and try on your own, use the `TEA-Book-Samples` launch configuration as usual and run TEA ➤ Samples ➤ CH09-S01: Statistics.

Note   To be able to demonstrate statistics output without the contribution, as previously shown, the sample code additionally ensures that the contribution is only added when the sample `TaskChain` for this chapter is run. As a result, the actual code in the sample project `org.eclipse.tea.samples.ch09.s01` will include an according check in addition to the code in Listing 9-1.

CHAPTER 10

Tasking Live View

The Tasking Live View is a central place aggregating status and progress information in a very detailed manner—much more detailed than the default Eclipse progress reporting.

Progress View vs. Tasking Live View

Figures 10-1 and 10-2 compare the level of detail in default Eclipse progress and Tasking Live View reporting. You can open both views by searching for them in the Quick Access text box in the upper-right corner of the IDE. Be sure to run a runtime workspace (for example, run the TEA-Book-Samples launch configuration).

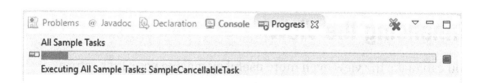

Figure 10-1. *Eclipse built-in progress reporting*

© Markus Duft 2018
M. Duft, *Eclipse TEA Revealed*, https://doi.org/10.1007/978-1-4842-4093-9_10

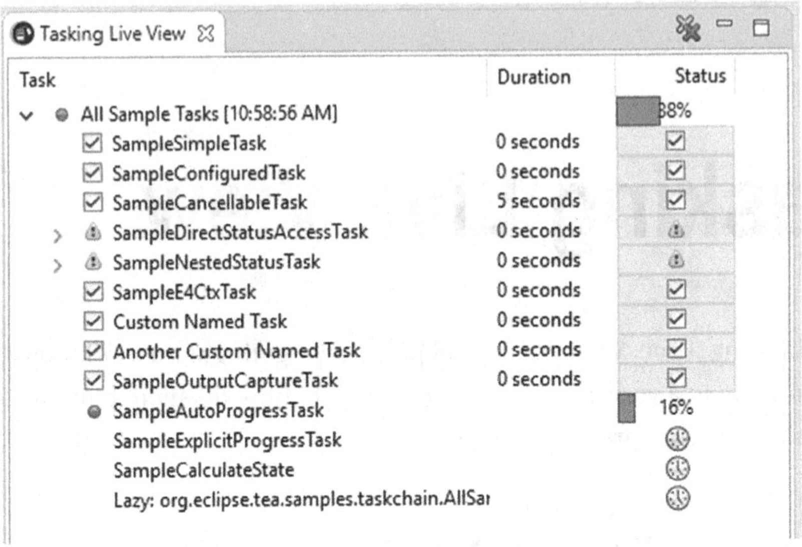

Figure 10-2. Tasking Live View progress reporting

The Tasking Live View can report nested status elements to unlimited depth in theory (see Chapter 8). It uses the IStatus returned by the Task executed directly, so you can directly influence what is shown in the view.

Enhancing the View

You can make the view even more useful by making your Task return MarkerStatus objects (which is an IStatus with an attached IMarker). For instance, the org.eclipse.tea.library.build.tasks.TaskBuildWorkspace does this. (We will look at this Task and especially at the component backing it in more detail in Chapter 12.) Figure 10-3 shows how the view will render a compile problem in a Java file. Double-clicking the node with the actual problems will make Eclipse jump to that location, just as implemented in Eclipse's Problems View.

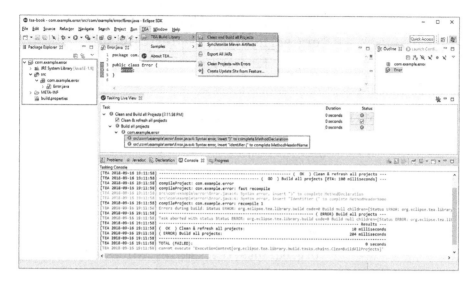

Figure 10-3. *Interactive status with MarkerStatus objects*

To try this out on your own, run TEA-Book-Samples (or any other TEA-enabled IDE) and create a plug-in project in the runtime workspace. Add a Java file with a compile error and run TEA ➤ TEA Build Library ➤ Clean and Build all Projects.

Leveraging this feature in your own Task is as simple as creating and returning a MarkerStatus (or a MultiStatus containing a MarkerStatus at any nesting level). (See Listing 10-1.)

Listing 10-1. Creating MarkerStatus to Be Able to Jump to the IMarker location in the Tasking Live View

```
public class TaskRunSomething {

    @Execute
    public IStatus run(TaskingLog log) {
            IMarker marker = getAnyMarker();

            if (marker == null) {
```

```
                return new Status(IStatus.WARNING,
                "org.eclipse.tea.samples.ch10.s01",
                "Cannot find any problem");
        }

        String location = marker.getAttribute(
                IMarker.LOCATION,
                Marker.getResource()
                        .getProjectRelativePath()
                        .toOSString());

        return new MarkerStatus(IStatus.WARNING,
                "org.eclipse.tea.samples.ch10.s01",
                "Double-click to go to " +
                location + ")", marker);
    }

    private IMarker getAnyMarker() {
        try {
            return ResourcesPlugin
                    .getWorkspace()
                    .getRoot()
                    .findMarkers(
                            IMarker.PROBLEM, true,
                            IResource
                                    .DEPTH_INFINITE)[0];
        } catch (Exception e) {
            return null;
        }
    }
}
```

This code will try to find (in a quite non-production-suitable way!) the first IMarker of type PROBLEM (regardless of severity) in the workspace. (When experimenting, make sure to have at least one warning or error in the runtime workspace. If you reuse the TEA-Book-Samples launch configuration with the com.example.error project from Figure 10-3 you'll be fine.) The example in org.eclipse.tea.samples.ch10.s01 contains the full code. Use the TEA-Book-Samples launch configuration to run it— use TEA ➤ Samples ➤ CH10-S01: MarkerStatus.

The MarkerStatus will lead to an interactive node in the Tasking Live View, which when clicked will make Eclipse jump to that IMarker's associated IResource – this is shown in Figure 10-4.

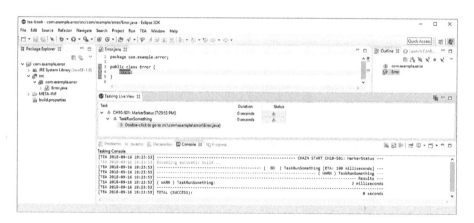

Figure 10-4. *Custom MarkerStatus in Tasking Live View*

> **Note**   Depending on the OS and Eclipse version, you might need to open (activate) the Tasking Live View once before it will start to pick up TEA events. This has to happen before starting execution of a TaskChain because already running executions will not be picked up when the view is initialized. This is due to the lazy initialization mechanisms Eclipse uses to save resources by not creating views that are currently not required.

CHAPTER 11

E4 Events

TEA provides a bridge from its own `TaskingLifeCycleListener` mechanism to the E4[1] event bus mechanism. This allows for some advanced integration in a more Eclipse-ish fashion. Actually, the `Tasking Live View` is implemented based on this mechanism. It is a plain E4 view part that requests TEA events from the Eclipse event bus.

The Event Bridge

The bridge is implemented in `org.eclipse.tea.core.ui.internal.listeners.EventBrokerBridge`. It is quite straightforward since it broadcasts an event for every `TaskingLifeCycleListener` method possible to the Eclipse `IEventBroker`. TEA uses the `org/eclipse/tea/*` topic namespace for this.

---

[1]E4 is the name of the new APIs introduced with Eclipse 4+

© Markus Duft 2018
M. Duft, *Eclipse TEA Revealed*, https://doi.org/10.1007/978-1-4842-4093-9_11

Note   You can spy on these events using Eclipse's E4 tools, which can be found in the marketplace.[2] Figure 11-1 shows an example of this. Once installed (in the TEA workspace, not the runtime workspace), the event spy can be accessed from (in the runtime workspace, when using the TEA-Book-Samples launch configuration) Window ➤ Spies ➤ Event Spy.

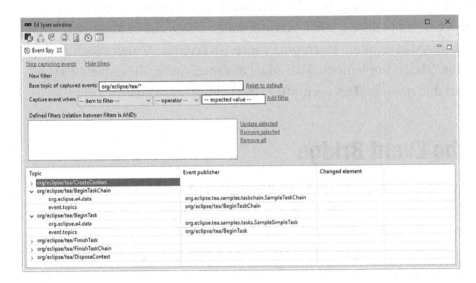

Figure 11-1. *Using the E4 Event Spy to see TEA events on the Eclipse event bus*

Every event sent by the bridge component has the currently active IEclipseContext used by TEA for dependency injection of TEA components attached as data object. This allows extracting anything in the TEA DI context as well as "resuming" the DI chain when receiving an event, as shown in Listing 11-1.

---

[2]https://marketplace.eclipse.org/content/eclipse-4-tools-event-spy

Listing 11-1. Subscribing to and Processing TEA Events

```
@Component(immediate = true)
public class SampleE4EventListener
                    implements EventHandler {

    @Activate
    public void activate() {
        IEventBroker broker = E4Workbench
            .getServiceContext()
            .get(IEventBroker.class);
        broker.subscribe(
            EventBrokerBridge.EVENT_TOPIC_BASE
            + "*", null,
            SampleE4EventListener.this, true);
    }

    @Override
    public void handleEvent(Event event) {
        Object data = event
            .getProperty(IEventBroker.DATA);
        if (!(data instanceof IEclipseContext)) {
            return;
        }
        IEclipseContext eventContext =
            (IEclipseContext) data;

        // show events for this
        // sample project only.
        if (!eventContext.get(TaskChain.class)
                .getClass().getName()
                .contains("ch11.s01")) {
            return;
```

```
                    }
                    IEclipseContext child = eventContext
                            .createChild(
                                    "My Processing Context");

                    child.set(Event.class, event);

                    ContextInjectionFactory
                            .invoke(this, Execute.class, child);
            }

            @Execute
            public void process(
                                    TaskingLog log, Event event) {
                    log.info("received " + event);
            }

    }
```

This code shows how to quickly and dirtily attach a listener to the events. To see this live, run TEA ➤ Samples ➤ CH11-S01: E4 Events in the runtime workspace of TEA-Book-Samples, as demonstrated in Figure 11-2.

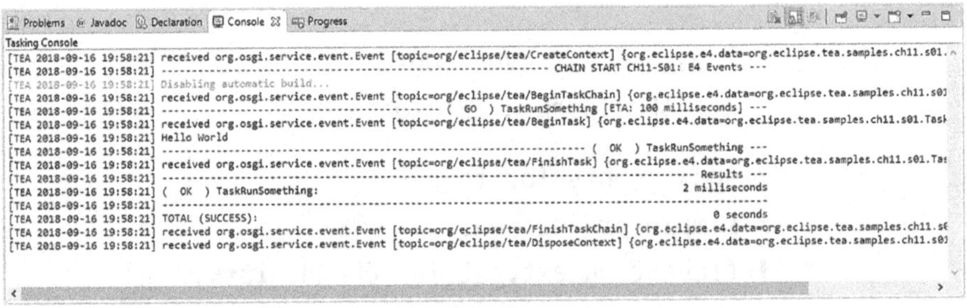

Figure 11-2. *Custom component to capture TEA events in action*

In a typical E4 application (or Eclipse plug-in), you will likely implement E4 objects that can use DI to obtain the IEventBroker for the application. In this example, we're using an OSGi service that is activated on plug-in activation (due to the immediate attribute). Right there in the @Activate method (another OSGi declarative service annotation), we subscribe to all TEA events (providing the service itself as event handler).

The handleEvent method is now called for every event that matches the filter given to the IEventBroker when calling the subscribe method. We briefly check whether the Event instance looks like we expect it. Then we create a child context of the associated context. (This is the current IEclipseContext in use by TEA. Depending on the event, this can be either of the previously described IEclipseContext levels in the context stack used by TEA.) We need this context to be able to add things to it without interfering with TEA itself. Now we can stuff the current Event instance in the child context and use E4's DI mechanism to invoke the process method by telling the framework to invoke a method annotated with @Execute on this.

This trick allows us to get back to TEA's dependency injection mechanism because we're using the actual context (as parent of our child context). This will allow us to inject whatever is injectable with TEA as well as the current Event instance (as we added that to the context).

With the conclusion of this chapter, we have covered all technical concepts of TEA core (and core UI) as seen in Figure 3-2 back in Chapter 3. We'll now move on to the TEA library, which contains TEA component implementations for advanced use cases.

CHAPTER 12

TEA Build Library

The "Build Library" is a collection of pre-built `Task` implementations,
which can be used in your own `TaskChain`. As the name already suggests,
they are focused on build. This means there is code that can help in
compiling plug-ins, building update sites, and so on. At the time of writing,
most of the `Tasks` have a strong focus on Eclipse PDE[1] projects.

The heart of the Build Library is the so-called `TeaBuildChain`.[2] This
heart is responsible for orchestrating builds. A build may consist of
compiling projects (maybe containing a generator), running generators,
compiling more projects (containing the newly generated code), and so
forth. Virtually anything can be made part of a build—generating code and
documentation, downloading files, uploading files, and so on. It heavily
depends on what you need. Having orchestration on top of builds was—as
mentioned in the introduction—the initial reason for creating the TEA
predecessor in the first place.

The `TeaBuildChain` is usually used through `TaskBuildWorkspace`,[3]
which implements all the details around it. But `TeaBuildChain` can also be
used stand-alone or in other `Task` implementations.

Once started up, `TeaBuildChain` will discover a set of `TeaBuildElement`
objects. Next, it will discover dependencies between these elements. This
will create `TeaDependencyWire` objects, which wire up all `TeaBuildElement`

---

[1]https://www.eclipse.org/pde/

[2]org.eclipse.tea.library.build.chain.TeaBuildChain

[3]org.eclipse.tea.library.build.tasks.TaskBuildWorkspace

M. Duft, *Eclipse TEA Revealed*, https://doi.org/10.1007/978-1-4842-4093-9_12

115

objects with each other. Once this directed (hopefully acyclic) graph has been created in memory, TEA will figure out an order in which elements can be visited. All elements are assigned a sequence number. Elements with the same sequence number could be built in parallel, provided the underlying Eclipse builders support that—which is currently not (yet) the case.

In the final stage, `TeaBuildVisitor` implementations are called in order and allowed to process elements.

Note   In the default implementation, the `TeaBuildChain` will build PDE Plug-in Projects only, due to its strong affinity to them in its history. It is trivial to implement support for any other project type though.

Custom Build Elements

Let's see how these things could look in a very simple example. We will need four different components, each of them shown in the following Listings: 12-1, 12-2, 12-3, and 12-4. This might seem like overkill for this simple example, but looking at the skeleton of the four code snippets allows for a quick implementation of much more complex scenarios if required.

Note   You can find the whole code in the `org.eclipse.tea.` `samples.ch12.s01` project in the TEA workspace.

Listing 12-1. The TeaBuildElement Implementation

```
public class S01Element extends
                TeaBuildProjectElement {
    public static final String S01_NAME =
                        "generate time for ";
```

```java
public SO1Element(IProject prj) {
    super(prj);
}

@Override
public String getName() {
    return SO1_NAME + getProject().getName();
}

public void runGenerator(TaskingLog log) {
    File p = getProject()
                    .getLocation().toFile();
    try (PrintStream ps =
                    new PrintStream(
                    new FileOutputStream(
                    new File(p, "out.txt")))) {
            ps.println("current time: " +
                    System.currentTimeMillis());
            getProject().refreshLocal(
                    IResource.DEPTH_INFINITE,
                    null);
    } catch(Exception e) {
            log.error("oups", e);
    }
}
}
```

The code in Listing 12-1 represents the generator we want to run. It simply writes the current time (in milliseconds) to a file "out.txt" in the root of each project it is run against.

Listing 12-2. The TeaBuildElementFactory Implementation

```
@Component
public class S01ElementFactory implements
                        TeaBuildElementFactory {

    @Override
    public Collection<TeaBuildElement>
            createElements(TeaBuildChain chain,
            IProject prj) {
        if (prj.getName().contains("gen")) {
            return Collections.singleton(
                new S01Element(prj));
        }
        return null;
    }
}
```

This factory class will create a new S01Element (from Listing 12-1) for each project that has "gen" in its name.

Caution   When looking at the example that follows, don't confuse workspaces. The generator code we're just developing will run in the Eclipse IDE, which powers your runtime workspace. Thus, it will look for a project containing "gen" in its name in the runtime workspace, not the TEA workspace.

Listing 12-3. The TeaDependencyWireFactory Implementation

```
@Component
public class S01WireFactory implements
                        TeaDependencyWireFactory {
```

```java
@Override
public void createWires(TeaBuildChain chain) {
    for(TeaBuildElement e : chain
                    .getAllElements()) {
        if(e instanceof
                TeaBuildProjectElement &&
                !(e instanceof SO1Element)) {
            wireUp(chain,
                (TeaBuildProjectElement) e);
        }
    }
}

private void wireUp(TeaBuildChain chain,
                TeaBuildProjectElement pe) {
    // any project with 'gen' in its name
    // depends on its generator.
    if(pe.getProject().getName()
                    .contains("gen")) {
        SO1Element generator = (SO1Element)
            chain.getElementFor(
                    SO1Element.SO1_NAME +
                    pe.getProject().getName()
            );
        pe.addDependencyWire(
            generator.createWire());
    }
}
}
```

The dependency wires are created from each project with "gen" in its name to the generator that was created for the according project. In this simple example, this is wired through element names (which must be unique). In real-world implementations, more elaborate mechanisms to find matching elements could be required.

Listing 12-4. The TeaBuildVisitor Implementation

```
@Component
public class S01Visitor implements TeaBuildVisitor {

    private TaskingLog log;

    @Execute
    public void prepare(TaskingLog log) {
        this.log = log;
    }

    @Override
    public Map<TeaBuildElement, IStatus>
        visit(List<TeaBuildElement> elements) {
        return visitEach(elements,
            S01Element.class, e -> {
                log.info("generating in " +
                    e.getProject());
                e.runGenerator(log);
                return Status.OK_STATUS;
            });
    }
}
```

This last puzzle piece will execute all previously created generator elements. Putting things together we are now doing the following:

1. Creating an S01Element for each IProject (which represents a project in the runtime workspace) with the String "gen" in its name.

2. Making all the projects depend on their generator instance respectively.

3. Calling each of the generators. The visitor will be called by the TeaBuildChain at the correct point in time, depending on the calculated dependency graph.

You can now run the previous example. Simply launch TEA-Book-Samples again. Create new projects in the runtime workspace, one with and one without "gen" in the name—for example, com.example.gen and com.example.other. The type of project is not relevant for this example—anything goes. Nevertheless, I recommend using the type Plug-in Project here, so you can reuse the projects for the next example, which will require this project type. Now click (in Eclipse's main menu) TEA ➤ TEA Build Library ➤ Clean and Build all Projects. You should see output similar to that shown in Figure 12-1. Note the out.txt file, which appeared in the com.example.gen project. Rerunning will generate a new timestamp. Adding projects with "gen" in the name will generate an out.txt file for those as well.

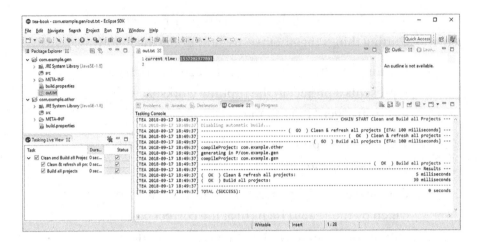

Figure 12-1. *Example output of demo generators*

There are two more tiny helpers in the realm of TeaBuildChain: The annotations TeaElementFailurePolicy and TeaElementVisitPolicy. The first one tells TEA how to treat a failure of the annotated TeaBuildElement. It can take these values:

1. USE_THRESHOLD: This is the default value. TEA will not immediately stop processing the build if any TeaBuildElement with this value fails. It will continue until another condition stops the build or a certain threshold of elements failed.

2. IGNORE: Simply ignore any problem with the element.

3. ABORT_IMMEDIATE: Immediately stop processing the TeaBuildChain.

The other annotation (TeaElementVisitPolicy) controls whether/ how an element is visited. It can take these values:

1. ABORT_IF_PREVIOUS_ERROR: If any element previously failed (even if the failure threshold is not yet reached), abort the TeaBuildChain processing.

2. USE_THRESHOLD: This is the default value. Visit the element as long as the failure threshold (the same as used by the TeaElementFailurePolicy) is not yet reached.

P2-Related Tasks

As mentioned before, TEA has a strong affinity to PDE and PDE-related mechanisms. PDE applications use P2 as the update mechanism. TEA provides prebuilt Task implementations that allow creating P2 update sites from any feature project in the workspace.

There is actually nothing you need to implement to make this work with your feature(s). Simply create one in your workspace and run TEA ➤ TEA Build Library ➤ Create Update Site from Feature.... You will be prompted to select the feature project to export (choose the one you created). (See Figure 12-2.) Now pressing OK will start the process of creating the update site.

Note   For this to work, you need a feature project in the runtime workspace. Create one by clicking File ➤ New... ➤ Project.... Select Feature Project and name the project com.example.feature1. Once created, open the new project's feature.xml and add the com.example.gen and com.example.other projects created previously in the Included Plug-ins tab using the Add... button.

Figure 12-2. *Select feature to export*

When executed, the TaskChain (TaskChainBuildAnyFeatureSite) will examine the selected feature. It will do the following:

1. Find all plug-in projects referenced in the feature

2. Export JAR files for each of the contained projects as well as for the feature itself

3. Run the P2 publisher to generate P2 metadata for the assembled update site

The site will be published in the workspace in the 01_BUILD_SITE directory by default. Since this directory is not part of the runtime workspace projects, you can see this directory only when browsing in the workspace directory using a filesystem browser of choice.

Note   TEA uses its custom configuration mechanism to provide the
`BuildDirectories`[4] configuration extension. It allows configuring
output directories for various use-cases via Eclipse's preferences
(see Figure 12-3), as well as in `headless.properties` files as
described in Chapter 7.

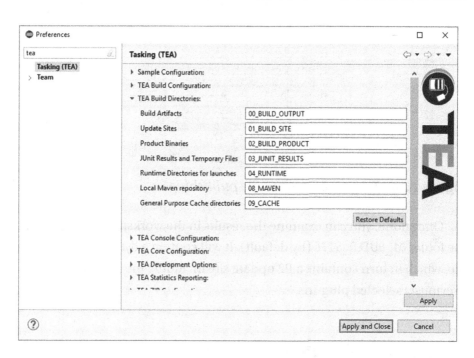

Figure 12-3. *BuildDirectories configuration*

The export process can be followed in the TEA console, as usual. It will
create output similar to that shown in Figure 12-4.

---

[4]org.eclipse.tea.library.build.config.BuildDirectories

Figure 12-4. *Output of update site publishing*

Once done, you can examine the results in the workspace directory in the folder 01_BUILD_SITE (by default). It will contain a `dynamic_site*.zip` file, which in turn contains a P2 update site including the feature and all previously selected plug-ins.

Maven Integration

TEA provides very rudimentary support for downloading Maven artifacts. This can be used for simple use-cases where single JAR files are required for plug-ins. More complex use-cases are hard to maintain (transitive dependencies are not fetched automatically). This may change in the future as TEA continues to mature.

The integration allows specifying a `MANIFEST.MF` header in any PDE project named `'Build-Maven'`. It can be used to declare one or more dependencies to maven artifacts. They will be fetched when clicking TEA ➤ TEA Build Library ➤ Synchronize Maven Artifacts or when running the orchestrated build from TEA ➤ TEA Build Library ➤ Clean and Build all Projects.

There is some initial configuration required to use the Maven integration in a workspace. TEA does not bring along a default configuration on which server(s) exist. This needs to be configured by providing a properties file containing the according server configuration. This file can be place anywhere on disc. It does not have to be in the workspace (although this is recommended). A sample configuration file is shown in Listing 12-5.

Listing 12-5. Sample Maven Configuration File: `maven.cfg`

```
maven_repo_type_DefRel00 = release
maven_repo_url_DefRel00 = http://repo2.maven.org/maven2/

maven_repo_type_DefSnap00 = snapshot
maven_repo_url_DefSnap00 = http://repo2.maven.org/maven2/

# Whether maven should be verbose or not.
maven_verbose = false
```

This configuration file can now be referenced in the preferences, as shown in Figure 12-5.

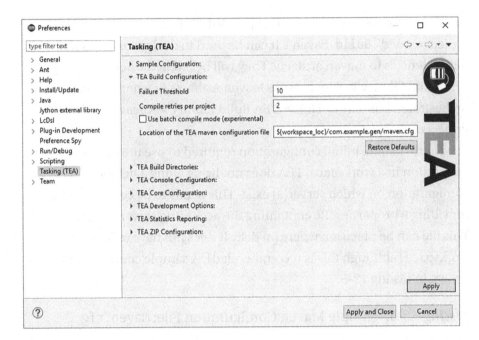

Figure 12-5. *Adapt location of maven configuration file*

Note   Eclipse String Variable substitution can be used in the configuration. See Window ➤ Preferences ➤ Run/Debug ➤ String Substitution.[5]

The configuration may contain an arbitrary amount of repository locations. They are specified by setting two properties for each repository: the type and the url. The mechanism is simple and straightforward: add the properties maven_repo_type_<NAME> and maven_repo_url_<NAME> where <NAME> is a unique identifier for the repository. Any id can be used.

---

[5]Usage is the same as variables in launch configurations; see also: https://
help.eclipse.org/photon/topic/org.eclipse.jdt.doc.user/reference/
preferences/run-debug/ref-string_substitution.htm

Note   Any specified repository is either of type release or snapshot. This means that a repository that should provide both release and snapshot artifacts must be added twice.

TEA will not automatically adapt the build path of the target project. This means that the usual process of adding a maven artifact is as follows:

1. Add the MANIFEST.MF header to the target project:

    Build-Maven: com.google.code.gson:gson:2.8.5

    See Figure 12-6 for a sample.

2. Run TEA ➤ TEA Build Library ➤ Synchronize Maven Artifacts.

3. Adapt the class-path of the target project. Use the MANIFEST.MF editor and add the JAR (using the Add... button on the Runtime tab), as shown in Figure 12-7.

```
📄 maven.cfg    ⚙ com.example.gen ✕

 1 Manifest-Version: 1.0
 2 Bundle-ManifestVersion: 2
 3 Bundle-Name: Gen
 4 Bundle-SymbolicName: com.example.gen
 5 Bundle-Version: 1.0.0.qualifier
 6 Bundle-Vendor: EXAMPLE
 7 Automatic-Module-Name: com.example.gen
 8 Bundle-RequiredExecutionEnvironment: JavaSE-1.8
 9 Build-Maven: com.google.code.gson:gson:2.8.5
10 |
```

Figure 12-6. *"Build-Maven" header in sample project*

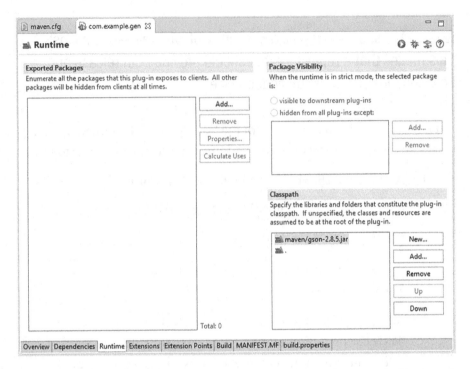

Figure 12-7. *Adding maven-provided library to the project classpath*

You can now access any code in the JAR from within the project.

Tip   TEA also downloads the source JAR along with the binary JAR from maven if possible. This allows setting the source path for easier debugging/source lookup. To do this, expand the projects Referenced Libraries node and find the library you just added to the class path. Right-click it and go to Properties. In the properties dialog, find the Java Source Attachment node. Use Workspace Location and browse for the source.jar. See Figure 12-8.

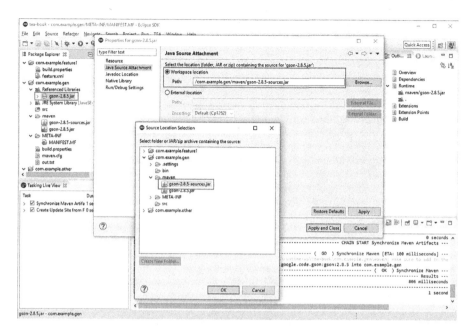

Figure 12-8. *Configuring source attachment*

CHAPTER 13

EASE Integration

EASE (Eclipse Advanced Scripting Environment)[1] is a very popular extension for Eclipse that has a similar focus to TEA's: extending the IDE. It can be used to dynamically extend the IDE using scripts in various scripting languages (such as Python—which we'll use in the samples, JavaScript, Groovy, etc.[2]). There are situations where EASE is better suited to extend the IDE than TEA—for instance, if users of the IDE should be able to change scripted behavior. Then there are situations where TEA is better suited—for instance when users of the IDE should not be able to change IDE behavior. And, last but not least, there are situations where a combination of both is the best solution—for instance, if users of the IDE should be able to customize parts of the IDE behavior in scripts. To summarize the main differences:

- TEA is part of the binary IDE. EASE scripts are (usually) part of the target workspace. This makes a huge difference in who can edit/change IDE behavior – and how much effort is required.

- TEA objects are written in Java (or any language that compiles to Java classes). EASE scripts can be written in various scripting languages.

---

[1]https://www.eclipse.org/ease/

[2]List of supported languages: https://wiki.eclipse.org/EASE/Engines

© Markus Duft 2018
M. Duft, *Eclipse TEA Revealed*, https://doi.org/10.1007/978-1-4842-4093-9_13

- TEA objects may access internals of the IDE when
  dependencies to these internals are specified. EASE
  scripts may access *any* class in the running IDE, as long
  as the containing bundle exports the class's package.

At my workplace, we use both TEA and EASE. TEA objects usually
provide the base framework for IDE extensions as well as default
implementations for TaskChain objects, which wire up these objects in a
meaningful default way. EASE scripts are then used whenever something
must deviate from the standard setup, or if there are project-specific
behaviors that should not be part of the default set of TEA objects.

TEA provides integration with EASE in both directions: TEA TaskChain
implementations can reference any EASE script and run it as if it were a TEA
Task, and EASE scripts can use the TEA script module to interact with TEA.

Executing EASE Scripts from TEA

Listing 13-1 shows a sample TaskChain that launches the script "/sample.py".

Listing 13-1. TaskChain Referencing an EASE Script

```
@TaskChainId(description =
                    "CH13-S01: Run EASE sample.py")
@TaskChainMenuEntry(path = "Samples")
@Component
public class EaseTaskChain implements TaskChain {

    @TaskChainContextInit
    public void init(TaskExecutionContext c) {
        c.addTask(
            new EaseScriptTask("/sample.py"));
    }

}
```

Now we just need to have an EASE script repository that contains this
`sample.py` script. Launch the `TEA-Book-Samples` launch configuration
once more, to follow along.

In the runtime workspace, add a new project. The project type is not
important for this project; you can use the general project. See Figure 13-1.

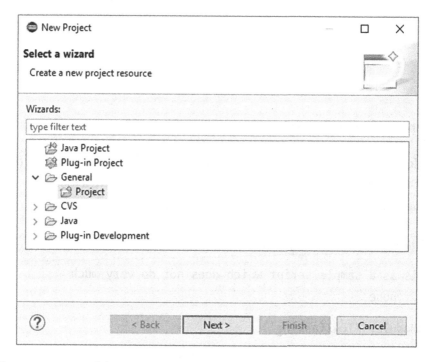

Figure 13-1. *Adding a general project to contain sample scripts*

The name of the project is up to you. I'll call it `com.example.scripts`
for the rest of the example.

Now go to Window ➤ Preferences ➤ Scripting ➤ Script Locations and
add a new workspace location—choose the new `com.example.scripts`
project. This is shown in Figure 13-2.

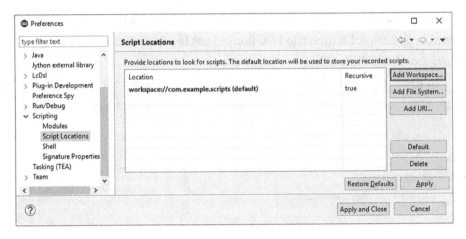

Figure 13-2. *Configuring script location for EASE*

Next, we need to create a simple script (`"sample.py"`) in the project. Right-click the project and select New ➤ File to do so. Have a look at Listing 13-2 for the content.

Listing 13-2. sample.py Content

```
# This is a sample script which does not do very much
# io : none

loadModule('/TEA/Tasking')

getLog().info("This is the TEA log from a script")
```

This script will not do very much. It tells EASE to not create a dedicated console for the script when executing (`'# io : none'`[3]). The script will use the TEA console for output anyway.

---

[3]Note that the '#' (which marks a comment in the python script) is intended. EASE parses special comments in scripts, see https://wiki.eclipse.org/EASE/Scripts

Now try running the sample in the runtime workspace (TEA-Book-Samples) from TEA ➤ Samples ➤ CH13-S01: Run EASE sample.py. You should see output as shown in Figure 13-3.

```
[ Problems  @ Javadoc  (l) Declaration  Console  ☒  Modules Explorer

Tasking Console
[TEA 2018-08-26 11:47:54] -------------------------------------------------------- CHAIN START Run EASE sample.py ---
[TEA 2018-08-26 11:47:54] Disabling automatic build...
[TEA 2018-08-26 11:47:54] -------------------------------------------- (  GO  ) EASE: /sample.py [ETA: 100 milliseconds] ---
[TEA 2018-08-26 11:47:54] This is the TEA log from a script
[TEA 2018-08-26 11:47:54] ----------------------------------------------------------------- (  OK  ) EASE: /sample.py ---
[TEA 2018-08-26 11:47:54] ------------------------------------------------------------------------------------- Results ---
[TEA 2018-08-26 11:47:54] (  OK  ) EASE: /sample.py:                                                      20 milliseconds
[TEA 2018-08-26 11:47:54] -------------------------------------------------------------------------------------------------
[TEA 2018-08-26 11:47:54] TOTAL (SUCCESS):                                                                    0 seconds
```

Figure 13-3. *Output of sample.py executed from TEA*

This mechanism can be used to call back to scripts in the workspace (which can be modified by the user) to perform customizable actions while executing a TaskChain that is otherwise not easily modifiable by IDE users (as it is installed in the IDE).

Executing a TaskChain from EASE

The opposite direction of the previous example is calling a TEA TaskChain from an EASE script. This allows integrating TEA wherever EASE supports integration for scripts. This includes (but is not limited to) dynamically creating toolbar or menu entries, reacting to E4 events on Eclipse's event bus, and much more.

We can reuse the already set up workspace from the previous example. Add another script to com.example.scripts: tea.py. The content is shown in Listing 13-3.

Caution   Scripts in this chapter have been formatted for readability. Please join lines ending with "\" when copying into the Eclipse editor. Otherwise, the script engine will not be able to execute it.

Listing 13-3. Content of tea.py

```
# Integrate with TEA
#
# name: Execute TEA Sample (EASE)
# io : none
# toolbar : Console
# image : platform:/plugin/org.eclipse.tea.core.ui/ \
             resources/tea.png

loadModule("/TEA/Tasking")

def myTask():
    getLog().info("This is a Task!")

runTaskChain(createTaskChain( \
    "EASE Sample TaskChain", [ "myTask()" ]))
```

You may notice that right after saving the content of this script, a new toolbar button will appear in the Console view of Eclipse. It is shown in Figure 13-4, along with the output you will see when pressing it.

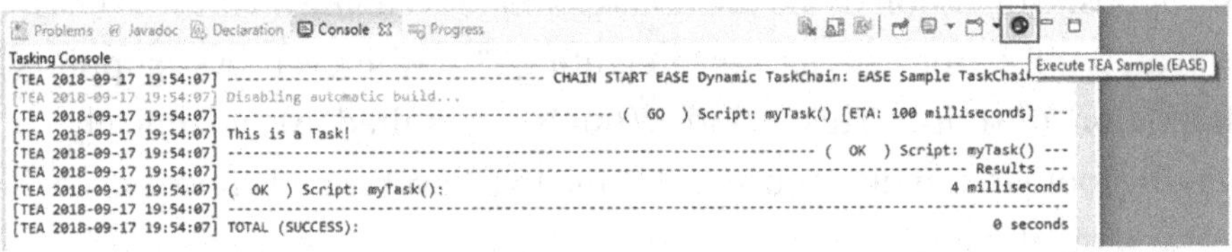

Figure 13-4. Button to Execute Script (Upper-Right Corner) and Output

The last thing to achieve with this script is to integrate it properly with the TEA menu in the main menu toolbar. Let's change the scripts headers (which are comments processed by EASE). Replace the commented top section of the script with the code shown in Listing 13-4 (again, remember to join lines ending with a "\").

Listing 13-4. Integrate Script with TEA Menu

```
# Integrate with TEA
#
# name: Samples/Execute TEA Sample (EASE)
# io : none
# tea : true
# image : platform:/plugin/org.eclipse.tea.core.ui/ \
            resources/tea.png
...
```

This will tell TEA that this script should be integrated in the TEA menu (the button in the Console View will disappear). The path within the menu is calculated from the script's name (note the "Samples/" in the name).

You can now execute the script from TEA ➤ Samples ➤ Execute TEA Sample (EASE). It should behave exactly the same as before when running from the Console View.

Following are additional TEA specific EASE headers (interpreted comments at the top of scripts):

- tea-dev : true: This will instruct TEA to only show the menu entry when Window ➤ Preferences ➤ Tasking (TEA) ➤ TEA Development Options ➤ Show TaskChains intended for development/ debugging is checked.

- tea-grouping : <groupingId> : This will instruct TEA to apply the given groupingId to the menu entry. This behaves exactly like when using groupingId field of the TaskChainMenuEntry annotation, as described in Chapter 6.

As a final example, let's take a look at how to reuse existing TEA object implementations from scripts. Adapt the tea.py script to have content similar to Listing 13-5 and rerun it from the menu.

Listing 13-5. Reuse of Existing TEA Objects

```
# Integrate with TEA
#
# name: Samples/Execute TEA Sample (EASE)
# io : none
# tea : true
# image : platform:/plugin/org.eclipse.tea.core.ui/ \
            resources/tea.png

loadModule("/TEA/Tasking")

from org.eclipse.tea.core.internal.tasks import \
    BuiltinTaskListChains

def myTask():
    getLog().info("This is a Task!")

chain = lookupTaskChain('CleanBuildAllProjects')

if not runTaskChain( \
            createTaskChain("EASE Sample TaskChain", \
            [ "myTask()", chain, \
            BuiltinTaskListChains ])).isOK():
        raise Exception("This did not work")
```

This script now demonstrates how to reuse Task and TaskChain
implementations from the script:

1. Use lookupTaskChain('...') to find any existing
    registered TaskChain.

2. Simply import any existing Java class by name
    and use it directly in the createTaskChain call to
    reference existing Task implementations.

TEA Event Triggered EASE Scripts

One more noteworthy thing: TEA provides a bridge from its internal
TaskingLifeCycleListener-related framework to the E4 event bus.
This allows attaching EASE scripts to certain TEA events. Try this out by
creating a new script ("event.py") in the existing com.example.scripts
project. Use the content from Listing 13-6 to kick off the experiments.

Listing 13-6. Reacting to TEA Events from EASE

```
# Integrate with TEA
#
# name: Samples/TEA Events
# io : none
# onEventBus : org/eclipse/tea/*

loadModule('/TEA/Tasking')


getLog().info("got event " + event.getTopic())
```

Now run any of the sample TaskChains from the TEA menu. You will
notice a lot of output generated from the event.py script,— as shown in
Figure 13-5.

```
Problems  @ Javadoc  Declaration  Console ⌧  Modules Explorer
Tasking Console
[TEA 2018-08-26 12:34:01] ------------------------------------------------------------------- CHAIN START Run EASE sample.py ---
[TEA 2018-08-26 12:34:01] Disabling automatic build...
[TEA 2018-08-26 12:34:01] ----------------------------------------------- (  GO  ) EASE: /sample.py [ETA: 100 milliseconds] ---
[TEA 2018-08-26 12:34:01] got event org/eclipse/tea/CreateContext
[TEA 2018-08-26 12:34:01] This is the TEA log from a script
[TEA 2018-08-26 12:34:01] got event org/eclipse/tea/BeginTaskChain
[TEA 2018-08-26 12:34:01] got event org/eclipse/tea/BeginTask
[TEA 2018-08-26 12:34:01] ------------------------------------------------------------ (  OK  ) EASE: /sample.py ---
[TEA 2018-08-26 12:34:01] ------------------------------------------------------------------------- Results ---
[TEA 2018-08-26 12:34:01] (  OK  ) EASE: /sample.py:                                           19 milliseconds
[TEA 2018-08-26 12:34:01] ------------------------------------------------------------------------------------
[TEA 2018-08-26 12:34:01] TOTAL (SUCCESS):                                                      0 seconds
[TEA 2018-08-26 12:34:01] got event org/eclipse/tea/FinishTask
[TEA 2018-08-26 12:34:01] got event org/eclipse/tea/DisposeContext
[TEA 2018-08-26 12:34:01] got event org/eclipse/tea/FinishTaskChain
```

Figure 13-5. *Output of event.py when executing any TaskChain*

CHAPTER 14

LcDsl Integration

LcDsl[1] (the Launch Configuration DSL) provides an alternative way to define launch configurations.

Writing a Launch Configuration

A typical LcDsl launch configuration for an Eclipse application looks like the one shown in Listing 14-1.

Listing 14-1. An Example LcDsl Launch Configuration

```
eclipse configuration Ch14_S01 {
    product org.eclipse.sdk.ide;
    feature org.eclipse.sdk;
    workspace "${workspace_loc}/runtime-ch14s01";
}
```

Note For a full functional description of LcDsl, please see its official documentation at https://github.com/mduft/lcdsl. For simplicity's sake, we'll just assume that it can generate launch configurations.

---

[1]http://marketplace.eclipse.org/content/launch-configuration-dsl

© Markus Duft 2018
M. Duft, *Eclipse TEA Revealed*, https://doi.org/10.1007/978-1-4842-4093-9_14

LcDsl will translate this code to a standard Eclipse launch configuration. LcDsl also provides an Eclipse View[2] (you have actually been using it all along to run the sample launch configurations), which allows convenient management of launch configurations. It is shown in Figure 14-1.

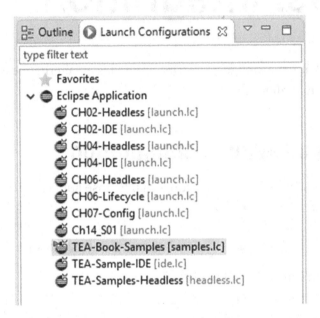

Figure 14-1. *The* `Launch Configurations` `View` *provided by LcDsl*

LcDsl has many features, which I won't discuss in much detail here. The official GitHub repository[3] contains more detailed documentation.

---

[2]`http://marketplace.eclipse.org/content/launch-configuration-view`
[3]`https://github.com/mduft/lcdsl`

Integrating with TEA

The most interesting thing about LcDsl is its integration into TEA. LcDsl and the Launch Configurations View bring along some API, which can be very handy when writing TEA Task or TeaBuildChain elements. Let me demonstrate with a short code snippet in Listing 14-2.

Listing 14-2. Launch Named Launch Configuration from TEA

```
public class TaskRunSomething {

    @Execute
    public void run(TaskingLog log) {
        LaunchConfig lc = LcDslHelper
                .getInstance()
                .findLaunchConfig("mylaunch");
        LcDslHelper
                .getInstance()
                .launch(lc, LcDslHelper.MODE_DEBUG);
    }
}
```

This code will look up a launch configuration named mylaunch in the runtime workspace and launch it. This code is not even TEA specific. You can do this from any code that has a dependency to the com.wamas.ide.launching and com.wamas.ide.launching.ui bundles (provided by LcDsl) as well as the org.eclipse.debug.ui.launchview bundle (provided by the Launch Configuration View feature), which is still pending review[4] at the time of writing.

---

[4]https://git.eclipse.org/r/#/c/93689/

To run the sample, you will have to create a new LcDsl launch configuration named mylaunch in the runtime workspace of the TEA-Book-Samples launch configuration. Launch it and create a new Java project, com.example.launching. Add a simple class named Test with a main method to the project—use the package com.example.launching. See Figure 14-2 for an example.

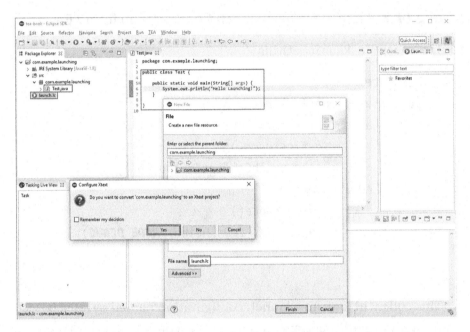

Figure 14-2. *Creating com.example.launching project*

Now add a launch.lc file to the project. Eclipse will want to add the Xtext nature to the containing project to allow "compilation" of the .lc file once you add the file to the project. See Listing 14-3 for the content of the launch.lc file.

Listing 14-3. launch.lc

```
java configuration mylaunch {
    project com.example.launching;
    main-class com.example.launching.Test;
}
```

Once you have added the content to launch.lc, try running a TEA ➤ Samples ➤ CH14-S02: Run LcDsl: mylaunch. You can also try running the mylaunch launch configuration from the Launch Configurations View.

The whole setup should look like the one shown in Figure 14-3.

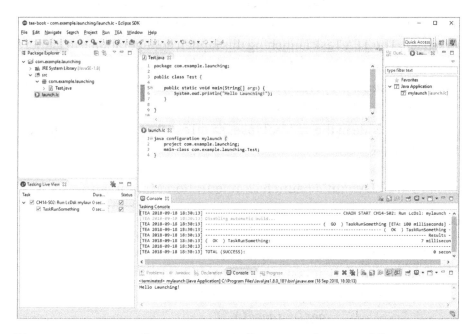

Figure 14-3. *Launching a Java application using LcDsl from TEA*

This can be very handy, especially in combination with the
TeaBuildChain extensions demonstrated in Chapter 12. Imagine having a
code generator that needs to read a model from disc, but the code to read
the model is part of your application framework. Thus, the generator is
consequently an application in your runtime workspace. The LcDsl API
facilitates launching such generator applications during builds. This is also
what the integration part is about. TEA provides TeaBuildChain extensions
that make sure that LcDsl-based launch configurations are available when
you need them during builds.

But the previous sample is not all. Even more useful is templating
launch configurations and building upon them in the code. By this,
I mean there is a base launch configuration template in the runtime
workspace. The TEA Task launching this launch configuration can gather
additional arguments at runtime, create a derived launch configuration
with the additional properties, and ultimately launch it. The code for such
a setup looks like the one shown in Listing 14-4. You can find a prepared
version of the code in the org.eclipse.samples.ch14.s03 project in the
TEA workspace.

Listing 14-4. Dynamic Launch Configuration Manipulation

```java
public class TaskRunSomething {

    @Execute
    public void run(TaskingLog log) {
        LaunchConfig lc = LcDslHelper
                .getInstance()
                .findLaunchConfig("mylaunch");

        LcDslLaunchConfigBuilder builder =
                new LcDslLaunchConfigBuilder(
                    LaunchConfigType.JAVA,
                    "mylaunch-new");
```

```
    builder
          .setSuperConfig(lc)
          .addVmArgument("-Dmy.prop=World");

  LcDslHelper
        .getInstance()
        .launch(
            builder.buildAndValidate(),
            LcDslHelper.MODE_DEBUG);
    }

}
```

The improved Task will create a new launch configuration (mylaunch-new), which inherits all the properties of mylaunch and adds an additional VM argument (-Dmy.prop=World) to it. This mechanism is not restricted to system properties; you can modify basically every property of the launch configuration (except its type).

Running the improved Task, of course, is more fun if you adapt the sample program. Figure 14-4 shows the whole setup once more. To try it with the prepared sample, run TEA ➤ Samples ➤ CH14-S03: Run LcDsl: mylaunch with property.

Figure 14-4. *Dynamically assembled launch configuration*

You may notice that the mylaunch-new launch configuration is
still kept around after execution. This allows manually re-executing
generated launch configurations. If this is not desired, replace launch with
launchWaitAndRemove[5] and the configuration is removed after execution.

Generating feature.xml Using LcDsl

Feature projects in the context of PDE are usually set up once and need
to be maintained—mostly to keep the list of included bundles up-to-date
with what is run from the workspace. This can be an error prone manual
task, especially since missing bundles may go unnoticed for a long time,
until QA misses functionality, or something of that nature. To avoid this,

---

[5]Take a look at com.wamas.ide.launching.ui.LcDslHelper for more API

TEA is capable of generating a `feature.xml` from an LcDsl launch configuration—actually, even from more than one launch configuration.

To get started, create a feature project as usual. Instead of manually manipulating the `feature.xml`, simply delete it. Don't forget to ignore `feature.xml` in your SCM—in `.gitignore`, for example. You don't want to/need to commit this file.

Instead of `feature.xml`, create a `content.properties` file in the root of the project. It must contain a single property: `dependencies`. This property must contain a comma-separated list of (existing) LcDsl launch configurations of type Eclipse or RAP (See Listing 14-6.) TEA will query all the required plug-ins (LcDsl calculates this from dependencies automatically) and generate a `feature.xml` from there.

Follow these steps to try it out:

1. Create a plug-in project, `com.example.bundle1`

2. In this project, create an Eclipse `IApplication`. (See Figure 14-5 for an example.) Remember to register the application using the `org.eclipse.core.runtime.applications` extension point.

3. Create a `launch.lc` file in the example bundle and paste the content of Listing 14-5. You can try the launch configuration from the `Launch Configurations View` now.

Note   Make sure the application ID matches the one in the extension point you created. Use content assist (default: CTRL + Space) if unsure. It will propose all available applications. See Figure 14-5 and Listing 14-5 for a working sample setup.

---

4. Create a feature project, delete `feature.xml` (only `build.properties` remains for now)

5. Create a `content.properties` file in the feature project. It should look like the one in Listing 14-6. What is important is the reference to the `MyApp` launch configuration created a second ago in step 3.

6. Now execute TEA ➤ TEA Build Library ➤ Create Update Site from Feature... (the same as described in Chapter 12). Select the feature project you just created and click OK. This should make a brand new `feature.xml` appear in the feature project. Additionally, a P2 update site for the feature is created, which already contains all referenced (dynamically resolved) bundles as well (See Figure 14-6.) Again, this is the same mechanism and result as described in Chapter 12, except that the `feature.xml` is now generated on the fly as well.

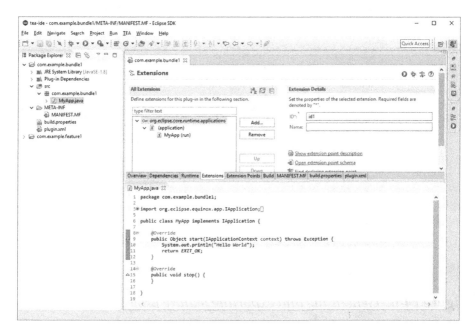

Figure 14-5. *Creating an IApplication in* `com.example.bundle1`

Listing 14-5. LcDsl Launch Configuration for the `IApplication`

```
eclipse configuration MyApp {
    plugin com.example.bundle1;
    application com.example.bundle1.id1;
}
```

Listing 14-6. `content.properties` for Example Launch
Configuration

```
dependencies=MyApp
```

Figure 14-6. *Generating and exporting feature project*

CHAPTER 15

Further Use Cases

What we have covered so far is actually the basics of TEA. The real power lies in bolting things together to form a complex set of `Tasks` and `TaskChains`. To enable you to get the most out of TEA, we will outline some more use-cases in this chapter. Not all of them will have the full implementation with them because some of them are quite specific to how your setup looks.

Accessing the E4 Context

Accessing the E4 context is a straightforward, yet powerful, "feature." Actually, it has very little to do with TEA itself; TEA just simplifies access to the context instance. The E4 workbench context can be used to access nearly every E4 object/service. For instance, Listing 15-1 shows how to access the current selection from the `ESelectionService`.

Listing 15-1. Accessing the Current Eclipse Selection

```
public class TaskRunSomething {

        @Execute
        public void run(TaskingLog log,
                @Named(
                        E4WorkbenchContextFunction
                        .E4_CONTEXT_ID)
```

```
        IEclipseContext ctx) {
        ESelectionService selSvc =
            ctx.getActive(
                ESelectionService.class);
        log.info("Current selection: " +
            selSvc.getSelection());
    }
}
```

As you can see, any `Task` (and `TaskChain`) can have the E4 context injected by TEA by annotating an `IEclipseContext`-typed parameter with `@Named(E4WorkbenchContextFunction.E4_CONTEXT_ID)`. As always, you can try it by using the `TEA-Book-Samples` launch configuration and TEA ➤ Samples ➤ CH15-S01: Print current selection. I'll leave it to you to figure out some output—it changes with whatever you selected in the IDE.

Menu Grouping

We talked about menu entries (using the `@TaskChainMenuEntry` annotation) in Chapter 6. Since grouping can be a little hard to understand at first, I have decided to include the more advanced parts of the explanation in this chapter.

When you have a lot of entries in the TEA menu, it can quickly get messy. This messiness is the reason for grouping. A very simple mechanism for ordering menu entries would have been to let each `TaskChain` decide on where in the menu it is. This is not sufficient, though, since different combinations of available `TaskChains` are possible with TEA, depending on which plug-ins are available/installed into Eclipse. Thus, we have the concept of the `@TaskingMenuGroupingId`. It allows the creation of groups of `TaskChains`. Each `TaskChain` knows the group it belongs to. Each group can (but is not required to) know and relate to another group. It can also specifically reference the "ungrouped" group, which is the group where all menu items without any group will be put.

Listing 15-2 shows a simple definition of two menu groups, exactly as has already been shown in Chapter 6.

Listing 15-2. Menu groupingId Definitions

```
@Component
public class MyGroupings
          implements TaskingMenuDecoration {

    @TaskingMenuGroupingId(
          beforeGroupingId = NO_GROUPING,
          menuPath = { "Samples", "Grouping" })
    public static final String GID_A = "my.A";

    @TaskingMenuGroupingId(
          afterGroupingId = GID_A,
          menuPath = { "Samples", "Grouping" })
    public static final String GID_B = "my.B";
}
```

This definition will do the following:

1. Create a group "my.A", which will be located before all ungrouped menu items.

2. Create a group "my.B", which will be located after "my.A". This effectively places items in the group "my.B" in between items of the "my.A" group and any ungrouped item.

An important detail here is that the menuPath attribute must match the path attribute of the @TaskChainMenuEntry annotation on the TaskChain.

Since grouping can sometimes be hard to debug, TEA offers a setting to display the groupingId of each menu entry along with it. To enable it, turn on Show GroupingIDs before Menu Items in the TEA Development Options. (See Figure 15-1.)

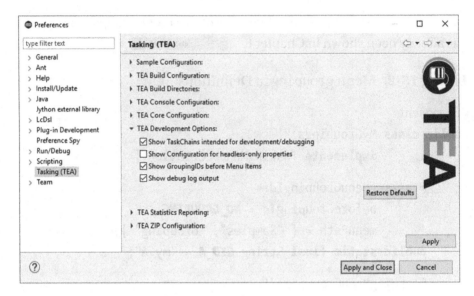

Figure 15-1. *Setting to show* `groupingId` *for each* `TaskChain`

This will change the appearance of the TEA menu. Each menu item will be prefixed with the `groupingId`, as shown in Figure 15-2.

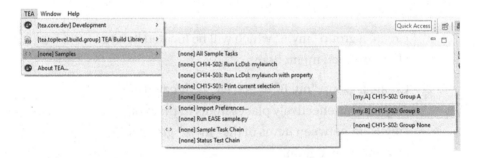

Figure 15-2. *Menu items with* `groupingId`

You can try this on your own in the `TEA-Book-Samples` runtime workspace.

Setting Up a Headless Workspace

I will now provide a very brief outline of how you would achieve setting up a workspace in a headless environment—at least how it is done at my current company at the time of writing. This outline changes from time to time, and there is no such thing as the only true way to achieve a workspace setup in a headless environment.

Setting up a workspace involves only a few steps. The actual code (which I unfortunately cannot share, as it is closed source) involves the following:

1. A Task that will detect a pre-cloned repository in the workspace directory. This repository is usually cloned by a Jenkins instance (using – in our case – the GIT plugin).

2. This Task will import a single hard-coded project from this repository. This project contains a file that describes the available projects, working sets, and so on. This can be as sophisticated as required, contain additional setup instructions, metadata, and so forth.

3. From there, the Task will calculate the projects that should be imported into the workspace. It will then use the IProject.create() Eclipse API to import those projects.

At this point, all projects are imported into the workspace. This is nearly the time to start building (using the CleanBuildAllProjects TaskChain).

The missing piece before doing so is the Target Platform. TEA brings along a tiny helper to set it: the TargetPlatformHelper, which is part of the TEA build library. You can use the code snippet in Listing 15-3 to set an active Target Platform from a .target file in one of the imported projects.

Listing 15-3. Set Active Target Platform from File

```
public class TaskRunSomething {
    @Execute
    public void run(TaskingLog log,
                    WorkspaceData data) {
        TargetPlatformHelper
                .setTargetPlatform(log,
                "test.target",
                data.getProject(
                    "com.example.target")
                .getProject(), true);
    }
}
```

This code will look up a project named com.example.target in the runtime workspace. (Make sure to create it or adapt the name if you want to test this.) From there, it will try to find a file named test.target and set that as an active target platform. It is sufficient to only have test.target; no other files are required. The test.target file needs to contain a PDE target platform.[1]

Note   The example code in org.eclipse.tea.samples. ch15.s03 (in the TEA workspace) is set up to be executable from the TEA-Book-Samples runtime workspace. This demonstrates once more that there is no difference between headless and inside the IDE, except for how a TaskChain is started (in this case from the TEA menu).

---

[1]https://help.eclipse.org/photon/topic/org.eclipse.pde.doc.user/ concepts/target.htm

The result (when executed from the IDE) will look like that shown in Figure 15-3, provided the project and file exist in your test workspace.

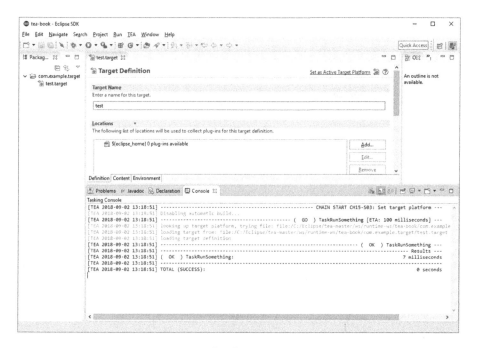

Figure 15-3. *Setting a target platform*

That's basically all that is needed. Now run the `TaskChain` `CleanBuildAllProjects` to compile all projects in the workspace. Of course, you are free to do more setup steps (such as connecting the resulting `IProjects` to the GIT provider).

Index

A

@Activate, 113
Architecture, TEA
    CDI, 33–34, 36
    components, 29–30
    dynamic menu, 36
    Eclipse project, 37–44
    engine and context, 31–33
    system components, 30–31

B

Build Library
    compiling projects, 115
    creating Update Site from
        Feature, 123
    custom elements
        TeaBuildElement, 116–117
        TeaBuildElement
            Factory, 118
        TeaBuildProject
            Element, 116, 119
        TeaBuildVisitor, 120
        TeaDependencyWire
            Factory, 118–119
    dependency graph, 121
    Eclipse PDE projects, 115
    generators, 121–122

IProject, 121
orchestrating builds, 115
running generators, 115
TeaElementFailurePolicy, 122
TeaElementVisitPolicy, 123

C

Clone repositories, 11
@Component, 42
Components, TEA, 29–30
    implementation, 34
    marker interface, 34
    system, 30–31
        interaction, 32
Configuration
    @Component, 80–81
    Eclipse preferences, 79, 83
    headless, 80
    headless.properties, 79, 83
    OSGi service, 79
    runtime updates, 84–85
    sources, 83–84
        PropertyConfiguration
            Store, 84
        TaskingEclipsePreference
            Store, 84
    task, 79
    TaskChain, 79

Configuration (*cont.*)
  @TaskingConfig, 80
  @TaskingConfigProperty, 80
  TEA preference page, 80
  user provided, 79
  values, 82
ConfigurationRefresher, 85
Console view, 45, 51
Context dependency injection
      (CDI), 30
  advantages, 33
  @Component, 34, 36
  component interface, 34
  context nesting, 35
  @Execute, 34, 35
  @Optional, 35
  OSGi component, 36
  SomeService interface, 33–34
  TaskChain, 35–36
  TaskingLog instance, 35

D

Declarative services (DS), 32, 36
Dependency injection (DI), 53, 64
Dynamic TEA menu, 36–37

E

Eclipse advanced scripting
      environment (EASE)
      integration
  createTaskChain, 138
  E4 events, 137

EaseScriptTask, 134
event.py, 141
execution
  TaskChain, 137
  TEA, 134
IDE, 133–134
lookupTaskChain, 140
runTaskChain, 138, 140
sample.py
  adding general
      project, 135
  content, 136–137
  script location, 135–136
  TaskChain referencing, 134
script locations, 135
TaskChain implementations, 134
vs. TEA, 133–134
TEA event triggered, 141
tea.py
  content, 137–138
  headers, 139
  menu, 138–139
  objects, 139–140
Eclipse marketplace client, 18
Eclipse TEA
  background
    build, 2
    code generator, 3
    Eclipse IDE, 1
    Eclipse RCP, 2
    headless, 3
    orchestration, 3
    workspace, 2
    WPoB, 3

FindBugs, 7

SonarQube, 7

tasks, 6–7

Eclipse TEA build library

    Apache Maven, 5

    build order, 4

    build scripts, 4

    Gradle, 5

    workspace, 4

Eclipse toolbar

    development mode, 68

    groupingId, 68

    icon, 67

    menu path, 67

    sub-menus, 67

E4 context dependency

    injection, 29, 155–156

E4 event bridge

    dependency injection

        mechanism, 110–113

    EventBrokerBridge, 109

    event bus mechanism, 109

    EventHandler, 111

    event spy, 110

    @Execute, 113

    handleEvent, 113

    IEclipseContext, 110, 113

    IEventBroker, 109

    subscribe method, 113

    TaskingLifeCycleListener, 109

Engine and context, 31–33

ESelectionService, 155

EventBrokerBridge method, 109

E4 workbench context, 155

@Execute, 42, 94, 113

Extension mechanism, 100

F

feature.xml files, 150–154

G

Gerrit server, 19

Git Repository, 19

Groovy, 133

H

handleEvent method, 113

Headless.properties file, 73

Headless *vs.* UI

    configuration, 73

    TaskChain

        configuration, 63–64

        identification, 65

    TEA workspace, 61

    updates, 72

    XVFB

        headless, 71

        Jenkins, 72

        SWT, 72

Headless workspace

    CleanBuildAllProjects, 159, 161

    IProject.create() Eclipse API, 159

    Jenkins instance, 159

    setting, 159

    target platform, 160–161

    TargetPlatformHelper, 159

I

IEclipseContext, 94, 156
IEventBroker method, 109
IProject.build() method, 4

J, K

JavaScript, 133

L

Launch Configuration DSL (LcDsl)
    com.example.launching,
        project, 146
    configuration, 143
    derived launch configuration, 148
    dynamic configuration, 148–150
    feature.xml
        content.properties, 151–152
        generation, 151–152
        IApplication, 151, 153
        project, 153–154
    Launch Configurations
        View, 144, 145
    launch.lc, 147
    launchWaitAndRemove, 150
    LcDslHelper, 145
    named launch configuration, 145
    templating launch
        configurations, 148
    Xtext, 146
Launch configurations,
    definition, 24

LifecycleAnnouncer, 96
LifeCycleListener, 85
Logging, *see* TaskingLog

M

MarkerStatus
    custom, 107
    IMarker location, 105–106
    IResource, 107
    Java file, 104–105
    MultiStatus, 105
    Problems View, 104
    TEA-Book-samples, 107
Maven integration
    adding maven-provided
        library, 129–130
    Build-Maven, 127, 129
    build path, 129
    Java source attachment, 130
    maven.cfg, 127–128
    process, 129
    referenced libraries, 130
    source attachment, 130–131
    synchronize Maven
        artifacts, 127
Menu, *see* Dynamic TEA menu
Menu grouping
    afterGroupingId, 157
    beforeGroupingId, 157
    groupingId
        definitions, 157
        menu items, 158
        showing, 157–158

menuPath, 157

@TaskChainMenuEntry, 156, 157

@TaskingMenuGroupingId, 156

N

Naming task

@Execute, 54–55

Live View, 54

@Named, 54

toString method, 55

O

OperationCanceled

Exception, 56, 92

OSGi runtime, 32

OSGi services, 29–30, 113

Output capturing

System.err, 57–58

System.out, 57

P, Q

Plug-in project, 37–38

coding, 41–42

@Component, 39

dependencies, 41

DS annotations, 39–40

Launch Configurations

view file, 44

launch.lc file, 42–44

LcDsl, 42

MANIFEST.MF, 41

settings, 38–39

TaskChain

sample, 44

Xtext, 42

Posts statistics, 97

P2 publisher, 124

Progress calculation, 87

Progress reporting

headless/console

state, 96

IProgressMonitor, 87

manual, 87–89

progress view, 89

TaskCancelation, 91–92

Tasking Live View, 89

TaskProgressEstimation

Service, 90

visibility, 89

P2 tasks

BuildDirectories, 124–125

export feature, 123–124

site publishing, 125–126

P2 update sites, 123, 126, 152

Python, 133

R

Restore Defaults

button, 81

Running Platform

target, 9, 14, 19

Runtime durations, 87

Runtime Workspace, 24

S

Sample Setup
  Clone Git Repository wizard, 21
  Git Repositories view, 20
  headless modes, 26
  IDE
    Console view, 26
    First TaskChain, 26
    launch configurations, 24
    TEA menu, 26
    toolbar of Eclipse, 26
  importing projects, 23
  runtime workspace, 27
  sample repository, 19, 22
  TaskChain, 28
  UI dependencies, 27
  workbench, 27
SamplePreferenceImport
  TaskChain, 63
Service component runtime
  (SCR), 32, 36
Source repository, 14
Statistics
  configure reporting, 97–98
  contribute additional
    information, 100
  contributions object, 100, 102
  custom statistics, 100–101
  JSON, 99–102
  @TaskingStatisticProvider, 101
  TaskingStatistics
    Contribution, 101
subscribe method, 113

T, U, V, W, X, Y, Z

Target platform, 9
  advanced mode, 11
  binaries, 14
  download Eclipse, 10
  EASE, 15
  Eclipse IDE, 9
  Eclipse installation, 9, 12
  Eclipse Marketplace client, 18
  Eclipse package, 9
  Eclipse TEA workspace, 13
  Launch Configuration view, 9
  LcDsl, 16
  Quick Start, 11
  source repository, 14, 19
  workspace, 9
Task
  dynamic name, 55
  implementation, 53
  IStatus, 56
  naming, 54–56
  output capturing, 57–58
  returning information, 56
  return values, 56–57
  SimpleConfig object, 82
  TaskProgressTracker, 53
TaskBuildWorkspace, 115
TaskCancelation
  Console view, 93
    IStatus objects, 93
    MultiStatus objects, 94
    Status objects, 93
  default estimation, 92

IEclipseContext, 94
multiple results, 96
multiple warnings, 95
runtime estimation, 93
Tasking Live View, 93
@TaskCaptureStdOutput, 57
TaskChain, 32–33, 36, 42–44
creation, 59
headless mode, 62
headless *vs.* UI, 60
identification
alias, 66
binary builds, 67
groupingId, 69–70
retries, 66
sub-menu, 70–71
@TaskChainId, 66
@TaskChainMenu
Entry, 66–68
TaskingMenuDecoration, 69
TEA menu, 68
runtime workspace, 62
@TaskChainContextInit, 59
TaskExecutionContext, 60
TaskingLifeCycleListener, 74
@TaskChainContextInit, 42
@TaskChainId, 42
@TaskChainMenuEntry, 42, 156–157
TaskExecutionContext, 93
TaskingAdditionalMenu
EntryProvider, 69
TaskingConfiguration
Extension, 73, 79
TaskingConfigurationStore, 83

TaskingHeadlessLifeCycle
@HeadlessStartup, 76–77
StartupAction, 77
TaskingLifeCycleListener, 109
@BeginTask, 75
@BeginTaskChain, 74
@CreateContext, 74
@DisposeContext, 74
@FinishTask, 75
@FinishTaskChain, 74
TaskingHeadlessLifeCycle, 76–78
@TaskingLifeCyclePriority, 76
TaskingStatusTracker, 75
Tasking Live View
aggregating status and progress
information, 103
IStatus, 104
vs. progress view, 103–104
TaskingLog
API, 46
Eclipse Console view, 46
launch configuration, 49
logging back ends, 45
OSGi services, 45
output coloring, 51
PrintStream, 47
stdout/stderr, 45
TaskChain, 50
Tasking Console, 45
Tasking Live View, 47–48, 50–51
UI implementation, 45
usage, 47
@TaskingLogLookupContext
Function, 46

@TaskingLogQualifier, 46
TaskingMenuDecoration
    component, 70
@TaskingMenuPathDecoration, 70
@TaskingStatisticProvider, 101
TaskingStatisticsContribution, 101
TaskProgressEstimationService, 90

TaskProgressMonitor, 91
@TaskProgressProvider, 88
TaskProgressTracker, 88
@TaskReloadConfiguration, 85
TeaBuildChain, 115, 122–123,
    145, 148
TEA Engine, 32, 59